Learning Resources Centre
Stamford College
Drift Road
Stamford PE9 1XA
Tel: 01780 484338/9

D1581142

Please return n or before the last date stamped be

'So You Want To Be Cabin Crew?'

By

Andrew D Porter

2nd Edition 2000 (ISBN 1 898129 58 4)
1st Edition 1999 (ISBN 0 9536232 0 3)

LEARNING RESOURCES CENTRE
STAMFORD COLLEGE
DRIFT ROAD
STAMFORD PE9 1XA

Published By:

Mach III
51A Sutton Court Road
Hillingdon
Middlesex
UB10 9HR

Tel: 01895 231 707
Fax: 01895 236 707

32607

WITHDRAWN

The author has made every attempt to check the accuracy of this book, but the author cannot accept responsibility for any inaccuracies contained herein.

ACKNOWLEDGEMENTS

The idea of putting a book together like this came to me back in 1998. Although it was more of a pass time than a serious attempt at writing a book, sales of the first edition made me realise that with a little more depth and a change of format the book could reach a greater audience. My thanks go to Paul Burge at Mach III for pointing this out to me and also for selling the first edition in his bookshops! Without his encouragement I would still be selling the first edition in its old spiral bound format via my web site.

Since I first set out to write this book I have been supported throughout by a variety of people. First and foremost Chrissie who has always been there for when questions needed to be asked and support given. I will be eternally grateful. The same can be said of my parents, Ann and Dave – thanks for all the proof reading and advice. Thanks also to Mark, Anthony and Jason, my closest friends, who have put up with me harping on over 'my book' for the last couple of years. Thanks also go to Airworld who gave me my first cabin crew job. Although they are no longer operating under the same name, I will never forget the friends I made and the great times I had with them – I don't miss the early starts though! My final thanks go to you the reader for buying this book, I hope it brings you success.

ACC	32607
CLASS	338.4791

CONTENTS

LEARNING RESOURCES CENTRE
STAMFORD COLLEGE

INTRODUCTION

You're reading this so you obviously want to be cabin crew! Hopefully this book will help you understand fully what the job entails and also how to go about getting one of the most sought after jobs in Britain today. As a former cabin crew member, I know exactly what the airlines are looking for when they are recruiting for cabin crew, and it is important that you do too. Overall, the aim of this book is to make you aware of what the job is about, and most importantly how to get through the application form and interview stages of the selection process.

My knowledge of the airlines and their recruitment policies has not only come from my experience, but also a lot of research which I hope you will find invaluable when applying for the position of cabin crew. It has taken almost a year to put this book together in a format that I believe is easy to read and understand. It takes nothing for granted, so if you're completely new to the airline world this book will be perfect.

So why does this career path appeal to you? Ask anyone what they think of being cabin crew and they'll probably say that it's an easy, glamorous job with perks such as stopovers in exotic resorts, cheap flights and holidays and the opportunity to bring home plenty of Duty Free. If this is what someone has told you, well they're wrong! Being a member of cabin crew is one of the most rewarding jobs I have ever done, but if you're in it just for the perks you'll also be in for one of the biggest shocks of your life. The truth about this job is that it can be really hard, dirty, extremely tiring and very unsociable. If you think you can do this job and still go out with your mates every Friday night then forget it! That said, the positives far outweigh the negatives, but I feel it's important that you should understand what you are letting yourself in for when you apply for a job like this. If you are rewarded with a position with an airline it is a job you will never regret doing, the friendships you build and the experience you obtain will benefit you for the rest of your life.

Airlines can be very particular when they are hiring new staff, hence the reason for the book. Each topic covered will hopefully make you so aware of what they are looking for that you not only have an idea of what to expect on the application form, but also it will make you more relaxed when you go on to the interview stages. Nothing is worse than walking into a room when you don't know what to expect when you're in there. Preparation is vital and this will become very apparent the further you progress through this book. Using it as a study manual is probably the best way of looking at it. Break each section down into modules and make sure you understand fully what is being said before you progress to the next stage. Admittedly some modules are very simplistic and you may ask yourself why you need to know such things, but familiarisation now can help you a great deal further down the line.

LEARNING RESOURCES
STRAFFORD COLLEGE
DRIFT ROAD

There is no guarantee that studying this book will get you a job in this industry, it is only a guide, but from the experience that I have I hope that I can help you obtain the job that you are looking for. I also felt that certain companies were exploiting people who wanted to be cabin crew members by charging them in excess of £80 for a day long course, which although very beneficial, I believed could be put into a written format. You also have to ask yourself why would you want to spend so much money on a course that provided no qualifications and no guarantee of a job at the end of it?

Many people work as cabin crew members, you will find a full spectrum of different people, but deep down I always noticed that each had an identical quality which shone through on every flight. This was the ability to be at ease around people, both the ones you are working with and also those who you are serving. Obviously each individual has their own qualities that they bring to the job and this is what makes working as a team in this particular situation so worthwhile. Before you apply for a job as a cabin crew member you have to ask yourself 'what qualities can I bring to this job?' Take a few minutes just to sit down and think what it is about yourself that makes you special and will ensure that the airline that you want to work for wants you to work for them. If you think you have the right qualities then go for it!

I really hope that this book is beneficial to you in your quest to becoming a cabin crew member. I wish you luck and hope that you succeed.

WHAT DOES THE JOB ENTAIL?

The job of cabin crew certainly suffers from stereotyping as was mentioned in the introduction, but I hope to clear a few things up so that you know what exactly you are letting yourself in for. To many people the job is that of a glorified waiter or waitress who has to have a permanent smile and healthy glow. It certainly is nice if you can smile all the time and look good, but glorified waiter it certainly isn't. How many waiters do you know can carry out emergency evacuations, have full fire fighting and first aid certificates and act correctly in pressure situations? This is exactly what this job entails and so much more. It may not be apparent now, but the role of cabin crew is mainly to ensure the safety and well being of the passengers to and from their destination. The fact that you serve them food, drinks and duty free are really just an added bonus to make their journey more comfortable.

You will realise just how important safety in this job is when hopefully later you start your training course and see that it makes up about 70% of the total content. The course itself is hard work and intense with lots to learn in a very short period of time. It wasn't untypical on the course I attended to start at 09:00 and finish at 17:30, but then to go home and revise all the material that we had covered for a test the following morning until 23:00! Revising for each test is so important as not only do you have to pass each test, the pass marks are set incredibly high so there is no room for complacency. Although the course is hard work, it gives you the ideal chance to meet some of the people you will be working with. Friendships created at this stage come in really useful for your first few flights as a familiar face in the crew room can make all the difference between being a nervous wreck and an over excited newcomer! I deliberately haven't included a section covering the training course as each airline will be unique, so you will just have to wait until you get the job to find out exactly what goes on.

The customer service aspect of this job is what is important to the paying passenger. The service that you give them is what will determine whether they choose to fly with your airline again or not, and at the end of the day if your service standards do not meet those of the airline then you will be looking for another job. For some people, dealing with the general public is second nature, for others it can be terrifying. Overall, they are people just like yourself who require you to provide a service for them. The public are nothing to be scared of! Developing a good level of customer service comes with experience, and in this job you will get plenty of necessary experience. If you already work in a customer orientated role you will find this aspect of the position easy. Those of you who haven't just need to be confident in yourself and your ability to do the job correctly.

To help you get a real feel for the job I have included a sequence of events for a 'typical crew member'. A lot of this may sound a bit confusing and complex at first, but as you read through the book it will become clearer, especially if you use this as a referral point later on.

1)   Check into the crew room.

Usually you will be required to check into the crew room at least an hour before the flight's estimated time of departure.

2)   Briefing of crew by the head flight attendant.

This is where the head flight attendant assigns the working positions for all of the crew members for the upcoming flight. It is then customary for the head member to test the rest of the crew on safety and emergency procedures which can either be specific to the position you are working, or to the aircraft as a whole. Once this is done first aid questions are asked and then the crew are briefed on the flight details and the order of service for the flight. Flight details will include things such as flight number, aircraft code, captain and co-pilot names, estimated time of departure and arrival for both legs of the flight and also any information that is specific to the passengers that are being carried. Such information may relate to the fact that one of the passengers is a diabetic or even the fact that they are a nervous flier. Information like this is vital to a cabin crew member as it enables them to react quicker to a potentially dangerous situation that may occur.

3)   Proceed to the aircraft.

Ensure that you have collected everything that is needed for the flight and along with the rest of the crew you will proceed to the aircraft. How you get to the aircraft all depends upon which airline you work for and which airport you are based. With some airlines you will have to walk from your base to the aircraft where as others have crew buses. Keep your fingers crossed that you end up working for an airline that has a crew bus as the last thing you want after a long flight is a lengthy walk back to the crew room upon your return!

4)   Board the aircraft.
5)   Carry out designated pre-flight duties.

The pre-flight duties that you carry out will be dependant upon which position you are working in during the flight. Such tasks will include ensuring that the safety equipment is in order, carrying out safety checks and checking that all meals and other essentials are loaded on to the aircraft before the passengers are allowed to embark.

6)   Stand at required position in cabin whilst passengers are boarding.

Each cabin crew member will have a position on the aircraft to stand in to ensure that the passengers are seated in the right places and also to help them with any of the hand luggage that they have brought on board. It is also important that any infants (under the age of 2) have an infant seat belt which is fitted to the guardians seat belt and that it is fitted correctly.

4

7)   Check all seat belts are fastened and ensure that cabin is 'secure'.
Each cabin crew member will then check that all the seat belts are fastened within the section of the plane that they are responsible for. During this check it is also the cabin crew's job to ensure that the cabin is 'secure'. This means that there are no hazardous pieces of luggage, all tables are correctly stowed away and that window blinds are open.

8)   Carry out safety demonstration.
Each crew member will carry out this task in a designated position on the aircraft. The first time you do this you will find it a pretty nerve wracking experience, but once you have done it a few times the nerves disappear!

9)   Take up position in crew seat.
10)   On orders from captain, begin flight duties.
Once the aircraft has reached a certain altitude and the captain believes that it is safe, they will indicate to the crew that it is OK to commence flight duties. From here the flight follows a set pattern depending upon the length of the flight. A typical order of service would be in-flight magazine, drinks, meal, tea & coffee, selling of on-board goods and perhaps a final drinks service. Again, each crew member is responsible for their own particular section of the aircraft when the service are being carried out. It is important to stress that a cabin crew member must be vigilant at all times, keeping an eye open for potential hazards and safety regulations that aren't being adhered to during all stages of the flight.

11)   Re-take seat for landing.
12)   Take up relevant position for passenger disembarkation.
13)   Complete turn around duties.
The duties that will be required of you will definitely vary from airline to airline and aircraft to aircraft. Some of the tasks that you may have to carry out are the re-loading of the ovens for the in-bound sector, replenishing the toiletries and checking for any left luggage.

14)   Repeat stages 7 through to 10 for in-bound sector.
15)   Crew disembarks.
16)   Proceed through customs.
17)   Debrief in the crew room.
This is where the post flight duties are carried out. This may include tasks such as completing the paperwork for goods sold on the flight and also counting monies taken. It is also at this point that you get the chance to discuss how you felt the flight went and to air any problems that you may have encountered.

At this stage you should still want to be cabin crew! Obviously there is a lot that you will need to learn and understand before you apply to become a cabin crew member, so now lets move on to see what the basic qualifications are and get the process rolling.

BASIC QUALIFICATIONS

Although there are some variations between company's, the following is a general list taken from one of the major UK airlines that you will have to adhere to if you are to become cabin crew. If you don't meet their requirements then it is unlikely that you will be considered. Non-UK based airlines may have different criteria - their requirements are usually detailed in the information that is sent out to you with the application form.

Age:

This can range between 19 and 41 years on commencement date.

Height:

Minimum of 5ft 2 inches to 6ft 1 inch without shoes.

Weight:

Refer to the following guide for approximate details.

HEIGHT	WEIGHT			
	Minimum Female	Maximum Female	Minimum Male	Maximum Male
5' 2"	7 Stones 2lbs.	9 Stones 2lbs.	8 Stones 0lbs.	10 Stones 0 lbs.
5' 3"	7 Stones 8 lbs.	9 Stones 8 lbs.	8 Stones 2 lbs.	10 Stones 3 lbs.
5' 4"	7 Stones 10lbs.	9 Stones 10lbs.	8 Stones 5lbs.	10 Stones 5 lbs.
5' 5"	7 Stones 13 lbs.	10 Stones 2 lbs.	8 Stones 8 lbs.	10 Stones 10 lbs.
5' 6"	8 Stones 1 lb.	10 Stones 4 lbs.	8 Stones 10 lbs.	11 Stones 0 lbs.
5' 7"	8 Stones 5 lbs.	10 Stones 7 lbs.	9 Stones 0 lbs.	11 Stones 6 lbs.
5' 8"	8 Stones 9 lbs.	10 Stones 12 lbs.	9 Stones 4 lbs.	11 Stones 9 lbs.
5' 9"	8 Stones 13 lbs.	11 Stones 2 lbs.	9 Stones 8 lbs.	11 Stones 13 lbs.
5' 10"	9 Stones 3 lbs	11 Stones 7 lbs	9 Stones 13 lbs	12 Stones 4 lbs.
5'11"	9 Stones 8 lbs.	11 Stones 11 lbs.	10 Stones 3 lbs.	12 Stones 8 lbs.
6' 0"	9 Stones 12 lbs.	12 Stones 2 lbs.	10 Stones 6 lbs.	12 Stones 11 lbs.
6' 1"	10 Stones 3 lbs.	12 Stones 6 lbs.	10 Stones 10 lbs.	13 Stones 5 lbs.

Appearance:

Neat, presentable appearance with the ability to wear the company uniform is essential.
Well cared for nails and hands

Hair - Clean and natural style
Complexion - Good
Visible tattoos are not acceptable
Stewards - No beards
Stewardesses - Make-up subtle and effective

Health:

Excellent health and hearing.
Good eyesight is required.
(If you take up a position, vaccinations may be required)

Education:

Education standard to O Level or equivalent.
Nursing, First Aid and a foreign language are useful but not essential.
Academic certificates are required for presentation at the interview.
Clear diction is essential.

Nationality:

You must be in possession of a full Passport and there must be no restriction on your employment in this country. Airlines based in other countries have the same kind of criteria. Check with the individual airline before applying.

Work Experience:

Employment in direct contact with the general public and selling experience is an advantage. Therefore, if you have ever worked in a shop, café or bar this is the kind of experience they are looking for. It is also helpful if you have handled money in any of these jobs.

Residential Location:

You will have to hold a passport for the country in which you are working or hold a current work permit. Please check with the airline before applying.
Usually you have to live within 1 hour of the airport, but again this varies depending on the airline. It is important that you can get to the airport in the time allotted, so ensure that you can carry out this journey even during the rush hour. Unfortunately, you must have access to a car to get you to and from the airport. Although most UK airports now have good transport links, it is unlikely that you will be considered for the job if this is the only way you can get to the airport - public transport isn't reliable enough just yet.

THE APPLICATION FORM

There are a number of ways to go about getting an application form for the position of a cabin crew member. Airlines do advertise their vacancies in the national press and also certain magazines, but you can also write to them directly and ask to be sent one. If you respond to an advert in the press you may be asked to either phone or write to them to request an application form. When doing this, ensure you make a note of the reference number that may be displayed on the advert and include it in your request. If you decide to request an application form without responding to an advert, you can write to the recruitment department of any airline. The addresses for the major UK airlines and also some international airlines can be found later on in the book. If you do this, be sure to make it clear that you want an application form for the position of a cabin crew member, including your personal details such as address and telephone number.

The most difficult part of getting a job as cabin crew is completing the application form, as this can be the difference between getting the all-important interview or being sent a letter of rejection. At present, 85% of application forms are rejected - make sure you're one of the 15% who succeed. For this reason it is of the utmost importance that you spend a lot of your time at this stage planning how to fill it in and also doing it correctly.

Application forms vary from airline to airline, some may be only a couple of pages of A4, where as others appear to be encyclopaedias when they arrive through the post! Even so, they all demand the same kind of information in some form or another. Before you rush into filling it in and getting it back in the post, there are certain rules that all airlines adhere to:

- The application must be filled in your **OWN HANDWRITING**.
- Only **BLACK INK** is to be used.
- All writing must be clearly legible and done in **BLOCK CAPITALS**.
- Keep all answers **WITHIN THE BOXES** provided.
- Answer **ALL** questions.
- Multiple choice answers must be highlighted in the manner requested by the airline e.g. 'Circle preferred choice base'

Personal Details.

This part of the application form is usually pretty standard with the airline requesting details such as your full name, date of birth, contact name etc. It is important that every question, not only in this section but the form as a whole, is answered in full. Some questions only require you to circle or highlight in the requested manner the answer which is applicable but if you are requested to expand the answer by giving details, ensure that you do this, even if it is only a couple of words. If a question isn't relevant to you e.g. "What is your maiden name?" and you are male, don't just leave the space blank – write in 'Not Applicable' or N/A.

Photographs.

Most airlines will require 2 photographs. One a head and shoulders shot (passport style) and the other a full length picture. It is important not to just send any old photo in! Take a new photo of you dressed in suitable attire which will more than likely be the clothes you wear for the interview. If you can, it is worthwhile getting the photographs done professionally as appearance is important in this industry.

Education and Qualifications.

When listing your qualifications always put the exams in the order they were taken. If they were all taken in the same year then they must be written in alphabetical order. Always put all your qualifications down in writing no matter how trivial they may seem stating what type of qualification it is i.e. GCSE, A-Level, G.N.V.Q. etc.

Most forms will also have a space for you to list any other skills or qualifications that you believe are relevant. At this point list any First Aid, Catering or Language qualifications you may have, again stating the date the qualification was gained and what level was attained. Most airlines will ask your level of proficiency when it comes to speaking foreign languages using fluent, conversational and basic as their 'grades'. It is important that you are honest when answering this question as airlines, more so those which carry a lot of non-English speaking passengers, will test you on your language skills at the interview. If you are unsure as to what standard you may be it is always better to be modest when filling in you answer.

Employment History.

When listing your employment history always put your present or most recent employer first, and then list them so that your first job is listed last. Always include any voluntary work or work experience in this section. It is important to give full details of what your previous jobs entailed, what you were paid and also give the full address with postcode and telephone number where possible.

Other Personal Information.

For me, this was the hardest part of filling in the application form. You are given a blank canvas in which to convince the airline you are the person that they are looking for. Although parts of the information that you put down will vary from form to form, I always tried to open with the same paragraph hoping that it could catch their attention.

"The position of Air Steward appeals to me because I like to **work hard**, am **quick to learn**, and enjoy working as **part of a team**. I am **not affected** by working **unsociable hours** and am **very adaptable**. I pride myself on my **high standard of appearance** and also my **caring nature** which I believe are essential qualities for this position."

This is a simple but effective way of starting and includes many of the special 'key words' that the airlines are looking for (in **bold**). The rest of this section is down to you and your past experiences, but always sell to them the points which you believe are suited to the job i.e. if you have done any work dealing with the public put it in because they regard this as very important when choosing cabin crew. Another favourite for the application form is getting you to give an example of when you had to work as part of a team. If this question comes up, be sure to include what the situation was, how you as an individual contributed to the team, and also what you enjoyed about the team. What the airlines are looking for when you answer this question is somebody who enjoys working as part of a team but who is also able to think for themselves and act upon their own initiative. This is how they want you to work for them should you be offered a position. These are just two of the most popular questions to appear on the application forms but don't be surprised if you are faced with a slightly different question to answer. For example, a key feature of being a cabin crew member is to provide good service at all times, so you may be asked to recall a time when you either gave or received good service, but what is good service? I would define good service as an occasion where somebody goes out of his or her way to help you, being polite and understanding of your needs at all times. Can you think of an occasion that fits this description? Maybe it was in a restaurant, a shop or an entertainment complex. Whatever the situation, when writing your answer, be sure to make it clear that you understand what good service is.

Now, looking at the completed application form provided, note how the form should appear once all the details have been added. When you have done this, try doing it yourself on a blank application form. At first do it in pencil so that you can erase any mistakes and rectify them. When you are answering questions which require you to write a paragraph or two, such as those described above, it is useful to write out your answer on a separate piece of paper to make sure that you can fit the answer into the space provided. Don't forget, the answer must fit into the space – no attachments are allowed. To help keep the form neat when answering these questions, I always found it useful to draw on faint lines so that the text remained level. If you do do this though don't forget to erase them before you send the form off! Once you are confident that the form is filled in correctly (using the guidelines provided in this chapter), complete the form in ink and get somebody else to proof read it for you. You should fill in all your application forms in this manner before sending them off. If your application is rejected you have to wait in some cases over 12 months before you can apply again. It is also important to note that unless an airline requests one, you should **NOT** attach a curriculum vitae (CV). If you do, your application form may discarded straight away without it even being read. Don't let a simple error cost you your job!

EXAMPLE APPLICATION FORM

CABIN CREW APPLICATION FORM

DRAFT

PLEASE ENCLOSE A FULL LENGTH PHOTOGRAPH

PLEASE COMPLETE THIS FORM IN YOUR OWN HANDWRITING, IN BLOCK CAPITALS, IN INK

DATE OF APPLICATION 01/02/00

PERSONAL DETAILS

Surname SMITH

Forenames IAN PAUL

Address 1 MAIN ROAD
TRAFFORD, MANCHESTER
LANCASHIRE Postcode MA1 1PS

Telephone Number (daytime) 015 25347
(evening) 016 74352

Emergency Contact Name MRS ANN SMITH

Relationship MOTHER

Address 2 HIGH STREET
ECCLES MANCHESTER
LANCASHIRE Postcode MA2 2SP

Telephone Number (daytime) 013 35274
(evening) 016 52472

Date of Birth 10/10/75 Age 24
Marital Status SINGLE Maiden Name N/A

Nationality BRITISH Place of Birth LEIGH
Dependants NONE

Applicant must be in possession of a E.C. passport before employment.

Do you hold a current 10-year passport? YES/NO

(If not, state type/nationality of passport held)

Height 5'11" Weight 11st 5LBS

Minimum height 5 ft 2 ins. Weight must be in proportion to height.

Uniform Size — Male: Chest 40"

Waist 32" Trouser Length 32" in inches

Female: Top 10/12/14/16 Skirt No. 10/12/14/16

Do you wear spectacles/contact lenses? (please state which) NO

Normal vision without spectacles, contact lenses acceptable.

Do you need a work permit to work in the UK? YES/NO

Have you ever been convicted of a criminal offence? YES/NO
(Declaration subject to the Rehabilitation of Offenders Act)

If offered this position will you continue to work in any other capacity?
YES/NO
(Please give details) _____

ATTATCH PHOTO HERE

Additional personal details
Applicants are requested to tick the relevant boxes below to enable the company to monitor its equal opportunity policy. Monitoring is recommended by the Codes of Practice for the elimination of racial discrimination and for the elimination of discrimination on the grounds of sex and marital status. This information is used for no other purpose and will be treated as confidential.

Male [✓] Female [ ]

Ethnic Group

White [✓] Black-Caribbean [ ] Black-African [ ]

Black-other [ ] (please specify) _____

Indian [ ] Pakistani [ ] Bangladeshi [ ] Chinese [ ] Other [ ] (please specify) _____

Number of days illness during the last 2 years 2 DAYS

Have you any disability or had a serious accident, illness or operation?
(Please give details) APPENDECTOMY (MARCH, 1989)

Do you have any visible birth marks, scars or tattoos? If so where? No.

Applicants must be in good health to pass a medical examination and free from any contagious condition.

EDUCATION AND SKILLS

Schools Attended (From age 11)	From	To	Examinations (Subjects/Results)
ST PETERS HIGH HOWARDS LANE TRAFFORD MANCHESTER MA6 1SP	09/87	06/92	G.C.S.E's DUAL SCIENCE B B ENGLISH B FRENCH C GEOGRAPHY B GERMAN B MATHS C SPORTS STUDIES A

Minimum qualifications — 4 GCSEs

Further Education Place	From	To	Type of Training/Qualification
WINMEL COLLEGE PRESCOT ROAD TRAFFORD MANCHESTER MA6 3SP	01/92	06/95	A · LEVELS GEOGRAPHY B MATHS C SPORTS STUDIES A

Languages spoken, please indicate degree of proficiency: F — Fluent   C — Conversational   B — Basic

French   B   Spanish _____   Portuguese _____   Greek _____

Others (Please State)   GERMAN - C

Conversational standard in a European language is an advantage.

Do you: Own a car? YES/**NO**

    Have a current driving licence. Provisional _____   Full   YES   HGV _____   No _____

How long have you had a full licence? ___ 6 YEARS ___   Do you have any endorsements? NO

(Please give details) _____

Full driving licence and own transport is advisable.

Do you have any other skills/qualifications which you feel may be relevant?
(e.g. Nursing, Catering, First Aid etc.)

COMPLETION OF FIRST AID COURSE. (1997)

Basic knowledge of first aid is an advantage.

EMPLOYMENT

Present/last employer THE EARLY READING CENTRE

Address TRAFFORD SHOPPING PLAZA

Position STOCKROOM ASSISTANT

Starting date 1/10/99   Starting salary £4.00 PH

Leaving date 2/12/99   Leaving salary £4.00 PH

Reason for leaving/wanting to leave END OF TEMPORARY CONTRACT

Brief description of duties performed UNLOADING AND UNPACKING OF
STOCK, MAINTAINING ORDER OF STOCKROOM.

PREVIOUS EMPLOYMENT — please provide details of your most recent employer first

Employer	Position	Starting Date/Salary	Leaving Date/Salary	Reason for Leaving
BIOCON TRAFFORD MANCHESTER 0161 2487	DATA PROCESSOR	1/1/99 £4.00 PH	30/9/99 £4.00 PH	END OF CONTRACT
SANCO WORSLEY MANCHESTER 0161 84216	JUNIOR CLERK	1/7/95 £3.00 PH	30/10/93 £4.00 PH	CLOSURE OF COMPANY

Where did you hear/read of this vacancy? DAILY MAIL - 3RD JANUARY 2000

Please state dates when you are not available for interview NONE

How much notice does your present employer require? NONE

Please give dates of any holiday commitments in the next 12 months NONE

No leave entitlement during seasonal contract

At which of the following areas would you prefer to be based? (Please state order of preference — 1, 2, 3)

MANCHESTER 1   MIDLANDS 2   SOUTH EAST 3

GENERAL

Where did you hear/read of this vacancy? _DAILY MAIL_   Have you applied to Airking before? ~~YES~~/NO

IF YES, when _N/A_   for what position _N/A_

Please state dates when you are not available for interview _NONE_

Please give dates of any holiday commitments in the next 12 months _NONE_

No leave entitlement during seasonal contract.

Please state order of base preference – 1, 2, 3

MANCHESTER _1_	MIDLANDS _2_	SCOTLAND _____
NORTH EAST _____	SOUTH WEST _____	SOUTH EAST _3_
		NORTHERN IRELAND _____

State your reasons for applying and why you feel you are suited to the position of Cabin Crew

PLEASE REFER TO 'OTHER PERSONAL INFORMATION'
IN THE PREVIOUS CHAPTER.

ANY OFFER OF EMPLOYMENT MADE BY THE COMPANY IS SUBJECT TO SATISFACTORY REFERENCES BEING OBTAINED

Please give names and addresses of two referees; these should be previous employers, schoolteachers/lecturers or business or professional people who have known you for more than two years. They must not be relations. (Referees will not be contacted unless an offer of employment is being made.)

MR AN OTHER   MRS NA OTHERON
10 LOCAL LANE   75 LONG DRIVE
OLDHAM   ECCLES
MANCHESTER   MANCHESTER
MA11 2SP   MA4 2AP

Your current employer would be contacted upon your acceptance of offer of employment.

RECRUITMENT POLICY

It is the Company's policy to employ the best qualified personnel and provide equal opportunity for the advancement of employees including promotion and training and not to discriminate against any person because of race, colour, national origin, religious belief, political opinion, sex or marital status.

Declaration: I confirm that the information given on this form is, to the best of my knowledge, true and complete. Any false statement may be sufficient cause for rejection or, if employed, dismissal.

Signature _Ian Smith_   Date _10TH JANUARY 2000_

INTERVIEW

PREPARATION

FAIL TO PREPARE AND PREPARE TO FAIL!

So, the application form has been sent off and now its fingers crossed waiting for the letter to say you've got an interview. Use this time to prepare for the interview as the airlines can contact you and want you to go down to see them within 48 hours! You may ask 'What is there to prepare?' Well, you'll be surprised. Hopefully, this part of the book will show you what to expect and also how to pass the tests that lie ahead of you.

The most important piece of preparation you will do is finding out where the interviews are to be held and how long it will take for you to get there. The worst thing you can do is turn up late for your interview as punctuality and good time keeping are kept in high regard in this industry.

You will be tested on your Maths and General Knowledge, so now is the time to brush up on it. Most of us these days rely on calculators to do our arithmetic, but you will have to do all calculations manually. To help, there is a chapter later on in the book covering this topic.

The general knowledge test is the ultimate pub quiz! It is hard to know how to prepare for this section, but just make sure you watch the news everyday, know a few members of Government, a bit of Geography and also your currencies. For this reason there is a list of Countries, Capitals, Currencies and Airlines, and also a mini General Knowledge quiz. Make sure you know all this information off by heart, as it will be useful in the interview. It is also useful to know a bit about the company you are applying to work for. Although it is difficult to know everything about any one particular airline, refer to the Airline Details section of this book to find out useful details such as the airline's fleet, date of formation, main routes and departure points and also other relevant information. More details can be found in the literature that they send to you, or by writing to them asking questions you want to know. It is also possible to find out certain information from High Street travel agents and from the Internet (a comprehensive list of web sites can be found later on in the book).

MATHEMATICS

Every airline interview will contain some kind of mathematics, either in the form of simple sums or perhaps a sample stock take sheet from the end of a flight which you are required to complete. Nearly always there will also be currency problems for you to solve. Dependant upon which airline you are being interviewed by, you may or may not be allowed to use a calculator. For this reason it is essential that you brush up on how to do you basic mathematics. Although you may think that this is a simple task you have to remember that when you are in the interview you will be under a great deal of pressure to not only get the answers correct but to also finish in the allotted time.

With all mathematics it is essential that you lay out the problem with which you are faced in a way that is easy to follow from beginning to end with plenty of space set aside for working out. This way it is easier to spot any mistakes that you may have made when it comes to checking your answers.

Addition

If in the exam you were given a set of numbers like these that follow, how would you go about putting them into a format that allowed you not only to do the calculation quickly but also accurately?

203 + 9 + 4444 + 18

What I would suggest is to stack the numbers on top of each other so that the calculation looked like this:

```
T   h   t   u
            2
4   4   4   4
    2   0   3
        1   8
+           9
4   6   7   4
```

Notice that by doing this the numbers are arranged so that the units (u), tens (t), hundreds (h) and thousands (T) are in the same column. When it comes to completing the calculation you simply add one column up at a time starting with the units in the far right column and working left through the calculation.

For this calculation the 'units' column adds up to 24. The 4 units are recorded in the 'units' column and the 2 tens are carried across to the tens column. See how the 2 tens are recorded above the 4 in the 'tens' column? The 'tens' column is then added up in the same way as the 'units' and so on until the calculation is completed, not forgetting to add the 2 tens that were carried across from the 'units' column!

Subtraction

Subtraction calculations are laid out in the same way, but always ensure that the number from which you wish to subtract from is at the top of the stack. If you don't do this you will end up with a negative number. The following examples will show you how to deal with the 2 basic kinds of subtraction puzzle that you will encounter.

1.
```
    T   h   t   u
    8   9   9   9
-   5   6   6   6
  _____
```

2.
```
    T   h   t   u
    7   6   5   6
-   3   7   6   7
  _____
```

The first calculation is simple. As with the addition calculations we looked at earlier, we start with the 'units' column. 9 minus 6 = 3, so is recorded in the 'units' column within the answer section. Progressing through the calculation we find that the answer is 3333.

```
    T   h   t   u
    8   9   9   9
-   5   6   6   6
    3   3   3   3
```

This calculation was simple because all the numbers in the number 8999 were greater than the numbers that were being subtracted e.g. 9 is greater than 6 and 8 is greater than 5. When this happens subtraction is straightforward. But what do you do when you come across a subtraction that doesn't follow this format? As we can see from the second example above, this calculation is such a subtraction.

Starting with the 'units' column we can see straight away that we cannot take 7 away from 6. So where do we go from here?

```
    T   h   t   u
                4   1
    7   6   5̶   6
-   3   7   6   7
                    9
```

The answer is that we borrow 10 'units' from the 'tens' column. By doing this we are now taking 7 from 16 and not 6. This gives us a 'units' answer of 9. When we progress to the 'tens' column we must remember that we are now taking 6 away from 4 and not 5. This is because we borrowed 10 units for the previous calculation. Again, as before we cannot take 6 away from 4 so we will have to borrow from the 'hundreds' column. This procedure is used until the calculation can be completed. In this example the answer is 3889. The following diagram will show how the calculation should be done.

Make sure that when you do a sum like this that you remember to alter the numbers that you have borrowed from. As in this example, the 5 in the 'tens'

```
T   h   t   u
    1   1
6   5   4   1
7̶   6̶   5̶   6
-   3   7   6   7
    3   8   8   9
```

column has been crossed out and replaced by a 4 because a 'ten' has been transferred to the 'units' column.

Multiplication

For multiplication, again, stack your numbers into their corresponding columns, with the number you are multiplying by being at the bottom of the stack. As with the subtraction calculations, there are 2 different kinds of multiplication that you will come across. The first is where you multiply a number by a single unit, for example 18 x 7.

```
T   h   t   u
            5
        1   8
    x       7
    1   2   6
```

As with the subtraction and addition, we start with the 'units' column. 7 x 8 = 56, so we record the 6 in the 'units' answer column and carry over the 5 to the 'tens' column. The 7 is then multiplied with the 1, giving us an answer of 7 tens. Remember though that we have 5 extra 'tens' from the previous calculation so we must add these to the 7 tens giving us a total of 12. When this is recorded in the answer section we can see that the answer for this particular sum is 126.

The second kind of multiplication involves a multiplier equal to or greater than 10. This kind of calculation is more complex because it involves 2 separate sums. Lets look at the example 36 x 12 to see what is involved.

```
T   h   t   u
        1
        3   6
    x   1   2
        7   2
```

So, where do we start? We have 'tens' and 'units so we start with the 'units' column and multiply 2 by 6. This gives us 12. The 2 is recorded in the 'units' answer section and the 1 is put on top of the 3 in the 'tens' column. The 2 is then multiplied by the 3 which gives us 6 'tens'. We must remember about the 'ten' we carried over from the previous calculation so this is added now giving us a total of 7 'tens'. This is then recorded and completes the first stage of the calculation.

```
T   h   t   u
        1
        3   6
    x   1   2
        7   2
    3   6   0
    4   3   2
```

This is where we see the changes come about. We now have to multiply the 1 in the 'tens' column with the 6 and the 3. It is important that in the 'units' column of the answer section we put in a 0 before we start. This is because we are multiplying by 'tens'. Now multiply the 6 and the 3 with the 1 in the 'tens' column. This gives us an answer of 360. Once all the multiplication is done we have to add the two answers together using the principles described in the earlier section on addition. So, the answer to this example is 432.

Division

Working out division without a calculator is probably the hardest of all the calculations that you will do. Again, there are two kinds of calculation. Dividing a number which gives you a 'whole number' as its answer e.g. 5, and dividing a number which gives a number involving a decimal point e.g. 5.76

T   h   t   u   Unlike other calculations that we have dealt with, division is laid out in a different way. The best way to lay out division calculations is as shown on the left.

Now lets work out this first example, 56 divided by (div) 4. We have to look at the first number, which in this case is a 5, and work out how many times 4 can go into 5. The answer is once, so we record the 1. So what do we do with the 1 that is left over? This is transferred across to the 6 making the 6 become 16. Now we work out how many times 4 can go into 16. The answer is 4. This means that the answer to the calculation is 14.

The second example, 158 div by 12, is worked out in the same way as the first in that we need to find out how many times 12 can go into 1. The answer is none so the 1 is carried over to the 5 to make 15. 12 can be divided into 15 giving us an answer of 1 with 3 to be carried over to the 8. 12 is then divided into 38 giving us an answer of 3. But what do we do with the 2 that is remaining?

The simplest way is to put a decimal point at the end of the number that is being divided, e.g. 158.00. This enables us to carry the 2 across to the first 0. 12 can then be divided into 20 once with 8 remaining. The 1 is then recorded (remember to put the decimal point in the answer too!). The 8 can then be carried across to the next 0. 12 is divided into 80 6 times with 8 remaining. This procedure is usually carried out to 2 decimal places as we have done in this example, so this is where the calculation ends. To tidy the answer up we can apply the 'rounding-up/down' rule. This is where the last digit in the answer is either rounded up or down depending upon whether it has a greater or lesser value than 5. For example, the last calculation that we did had a full answer of 13.1666. If the answer is to be to 2 decimal places we look at the third number after the decimal point. If it is equal to, or greater than 5 we 'round-up' meaning that the answer would be 13.17. If our original answer was 13.164 we would 'round-down' meaning that the answer would be 13.16.

Percentages

Once you have mastered addition, subtraction, multiplication and division you can then go on to working out percentages (%). A percentage can be described as a hundredth of a number, so to work out what 1% of a number is you have to divide the number in question by 100. For example, 1% of 100 is 1 and 1% of 250 is 2.5.

If you were set the task of working out what 15% of 600, we follow the following procedure:

• Divide 600 by 100 to give us 1% of 600, which in this case is 6.
• Multiply 6 by 15 to give us 15%

The answer to this percentage problem is that 15% of 600 is 90. Once you understand the procedure, set yourself a few similar problems to make sure that you have got the hang of things.

Using what we have just learnt, we can then go on to work out percentage discounts. When shops have sales they frequently advertise '10% off marked price', but what price does this mean the product is now selling at? If the marked is £50.00 and the sale sticker says '10% off', using the procedure we have just covered, we firstly have to work out what 10% of £50.00 is. Once we have done this we have to subtract this answer from the marked price, so '10% off' in this case means that the product is now selling for £45.00.

Currency

The final area that we are going to cover in this section is currency – learning how to convert from one currency into another. Although this sounds difficult it really couldn't be easier! It is just a case of simple maths using multiplication and division which we have already covered. The only difference here is that you will be allowed in most cases to use a calculator.

If you need to know what £GB5.00 is in $US how will you go about working it out?

To start, you will always be made aware of how much £GB1.00 is worth, so in this example lets say that £GB1.00 is worth $US 2.80. Now we have this information it is simply a case of **MULTIPLYING** 2.80 by 5. This means that £5.00 is worth $US 14.00. You would use this form of calculation when a passenger wanted to pay for goods priced in £GB with $US.

When carrying out such a calculation use the following procedure to help you –

Price - £GB 9.00
Exchange Rate - £1.00 = $US 2.80
Price in alternative currency - $US 25.20 (9.00 x 2.80)

If you need to know what $US 30.00 is in £GB then it is simply a case of **DIVIDING** the amount in $US by the £GB exchange rate (i.e. £1.00 = $US 2.80). For example, a passenger may want to pay for goods on the plane which are priced in £GB with $US and wants to know how much his $US 20.00 is worth. Again we can lay out the calculation in a format similar to the one above −

Exchange Rate - £GB 1.00 = $US 2.80
Customer has - $US 20.00
Currency is worth - £GB 7.14 (20 divided 2.80)

It really is this easy to carry out currency calculations. Please note that it is very important to always state the currency and its origin when the calculations are being carried out e.g. US Dollars, Great British Pounds, Spanish Peseta, French Francs etc. This is because other countries may also have a currency called the Dollar or the Pound, so by adding the country to the currency it allows us to differentiate between them.

As with all of the maths topics that we have covered, the only way that you will become competent at doing maths manually is to practice, making sure that you stick to the methods shown. Now, using the problems provided in the test section, work your way through the calculations until you feel confident that you can handle any sum that is presented to you in the interview.

COUNTRY INFORMATION

A key part of your preparation is to familiarise yourself with countries listed below, their associated capital, national airline and also their currency. This is an important skill to have as you will be tested on it in your interview and will definitely use it when you are flying.

Country	Capital	Currency	Airline
Australia	Canberra	Australian Dollar	QANTAS
Austria	Vienna	Austrian Schilling	Austrian Airlines
Belgium	Brussels	Belgian Franc	Sabena
Canada	Ottawa	Canadian Dollar	Air Canada
China	Beijing	Chinese Yuan	Air China
Cyprus	Larnaca	Cypriot Pound	Cypriot Airways
Czech Republic	Prague	Czech Koruna	OK Czech Airways
Denmark	Copenhagen	Danish Kroner	S.A.S.
Egypt	Cairo	Egyptian Pound	Egypt Air
Finland	Helsinki	Finnmark	Finnair
France	Paris	French Franc	Air France
Germany	Berlin	Deutschmark	Lufthansa
Greece	Athens	Greek Drachma	Olympic Airways
Ireland (Eire)	Dublin	Irish Punt	Aer Lingus
Italy	Rome	Italian Lire	Alitalia
Japan	Tokyo	Japanese Yen	J.A.L.
Malaysia	Kuala Lumpur	Malaysian Ringgit	Malaysia Airlines
Mexico	Mexico City	Mexican Peso	Air Mexico
Netherlands	Amsterdam	Dutch Guilder	K.L.M.
New Zealand	Wellington	New Zealand Dollar	Air New Zealand
Norway	Oslo	Norwegian Kroner	S.A.S.
Poland	Warsaw	Polish Zloty	L.O.T.
Portugal	Lisbon	Portuguese Escudo	T.A.P.
Romania	Bucharest	Romanian Leu	Air Romania
Russian Federation	Moscow	Russian Rubel	Aeroflot
South Africa	Cape Town	South African Rand	South African Airways
South Korea	Seoul	South Korean Wan	Korean Air
Spain	Madrid	Spanish Peseta	Iberia
Sweden	Stockholm	Swedish Kroner	S.A.S.
Switzerland	Bern	Swiss Franc	Swissair
Turkey	Ankara	Turkish Lire	Turkish Airlines
USA	Washington DC	American Dollar	American Airlines

AIRPORT CODES AND NAMES

Although airport codes are something you learn as you go along, it is important that you familiarise yourself with a few of the more popular destinations. The codes are made up of three letters and are unique to that particular airport. Some codes appear to be self-explanatory e.g. MAN for Manchester, ATH for Athens and REU for Reus, but things aren't always this simple. For example, do you know where YYZ is? The answer is Toronto in Canada. It really is just a case of spending a bit of time learning the codes. To help you a list has been compiled of the most popular tourist destinations and also the major airports in England.

Spain, Balearics and Canaries

AGP - Malaga
ALC - Alicante
LEI - Almeria
REU - Reus
IBZ - Ibiza
MAH - Mahon

PMI - Palma (Majorca)
ACE - Arrecife (Lanzarote)
FUE - Fuertaventura
LPA - Las Palmas (Gran Can.)
TFN - Tenerife North
TFS - Tenerife South

Greece and Islands

ATH - Athens
CFU - Corfu
HER - Heraklion (Crete)
JSI - Skiathos

SKG - Thessoloniki
ZTH - Zante
RHO - Rhodes

Turkey

ADB - Izmir
AYT - Antalya
DLM - Dalaman

Cyprus

LCA - Larnaca
PFO - Paphos

Other Popular Destinations

BCN - Barcelona
BRU - Brussels
CDG - Charles de Gaulle (Paris)

MCO - Orlando
PRG - Prague
SFB - Sanford

UK Airports	Name
Birmingham (BHX)	Elmdon
Bristol (BRS)	Lulsgate
East Midlands (EMA)	Castle Donington
Edinburgh (EDI)	Turnhouse
Glasgow (GLA)	Abbotsinch
Leeds/Bradford (LBA)	Yeadon
Liverpool (LPL)	Speke
London	City (LCY)
	Gatwick (LGW)
	Heathrow (LHR)
	Stanstead (STN)
Manchester (MAN)	Ringway
Newcastle (NCL)	Woolsington

Of course, not all of the UK's airports are listed here. Find out where other airports are located and what their names and codes are. Such information can be obtained by going to your local library or on the Internet.

Just to make matters more confusing, every airline also has a code. You will probably have come across it when you have flown in the past as part of the flight number on your ticket. Eg. BY2433 would be a Britannia flight and the four digit number would relate to the specific route of the aircraft. Listed below are some of the other airlines that you might come across.

Code	Airline
AF	Air France
AIH	Airtours
AMM	Air 2000
BA	British Airways
BM	British Midland
BY	Britannia
CKT	Caledonian
EZY	Easy Jet
FCL	Flying Colours
JE	Jersey European

PERSONAL PRESENTATION

The personal presentation part of the interview is where a lot of people can really embarrass themselves and spoil their chances of gaining employment. It is important that you spend quite a bit of time preparing this section as it really can make or break you. Your employers will be looking for someone who is good at speaking in front of people in a confident and professional manner. After all, this will be your job! Communication skills are a real winner at this stage. So what are you going to say? Although there is no exact pattern of presentation, the following should give a rough outline of what to say.

- Start by introducing yourself. State how old you are and where you come from.
- Your current employment and what your role is.
- Your past employment and education.
- Your hobbies and achievements.
- Why you want to be a cabin crew member for this particular airline.

Your presentation may be something like this:

Hello, my name is _____, I am ____ years old and come from _____, which is near _____.

At present I work for _____ and my position within the company is _____.
In the past I have worked for _____ where I was a _____. I held this position for ____ years before joining my present employer in 19__.

I attended _____ school where I attained ___ G.C.S.E.'s. These included pass marks in both French and German. I then went on to attend _____ college where I studied _____, _____, and _____.
During my academic years I played a lot of different sports, with _____ being my favourite. I was also fortunate enough to be picked for the town schools team.

My present hobbies include _____ and I am a member of _____.

I believe that I am suited to the position of flight attendant with _____ because I like to work hard, both individually and as part of a team. I am also able to work unsociable hours having worked between ____ and ____ in the past.

There may not seem a lot to talk about here, but this presentation should last between 5 and 8 minutes. Obviously, you will be able to expand on the outline given above, but ensure that your points are kept brief yet informative. Make sure you really sell yourself emphasising all your strong points, but whatever you do, don't say you want to do the job because you like to travel. Only once in my short haul career did I leave the confines of the airport! Most of the time, you only have a 1 hour turn around period before you are on your way home again. Plan your presentation carefully and practice it thoroughly so that it is simple when you come to do it for real. It may help if you make yourself a few notes as 'memory joggers' so that your presentation is easier to remember. The easiest way to learn your presentation is to learn each section individually. Once you have mastered the first section, learn the second section and then try to tie them together. If you do this for each stage of the presentation it will make learning and remembering it a whole lot easier.

It is important to stress at this stage is that this is a **personal** presentation. The above information is to be used as a guide on which you can build your presentation around – not copied! If you stick to the example above you may run the risk of having virtually the same presentation as someone else who has also got a copy of this book!

For those of you like me have a strong accent and tend to speak quickly, ensure that you speak clearly and slowly. You won't be frowned upon if you have an accent as long as people can comprehend what you are saying. Eye contact can also be a winner. When giving your presentation try to make it look as though you are addressing everybody in the room, don't just stare ahead. By doing this you are making people pay attention to what you are saying because they will feel as though you are speaking to them personally. The most important thing is not to be frightened by speaking in front of people. Preparation at this stage will make you look like a professional in a crowd of amateurs!

UNDERSTANDING YOUR ROSTER

"Why do I need to understand my roster now?" I hear you ask. Well, believe it or not it is all part of your preparation, as familiarisation now with common terms will not only help you during your interview, but also when you start flying. An important procedure in the life of a cabin crew member is being able to read the information on a roster correctly. All times are given using the 24-hour clock, and to confuse matters further are always given in GMT.

The 24-hour clock for those of you who are unfamiliar with it is quite a straightforward procedure. Instead of there being a.m. and p.m., time is just continuous over a 24 hour period. For example, 3 p.m. on a 24-hour clock would be 15:00. The following table should make it clearer:

1 2 H O U R		2 4 H O U R	1 2 H O U R		2 4 H O U R
1 2 . a m	=	0 0 : 0 0	1 2 . p m	=	1 2 : 0 0
1 . a m	=	0 1 : 0 0	1 . p m	=	1 3 : 0 0
2 . a m	=	0 2 : 0 0	2 . p m	=	1 4 : 0 0
3 . a m	=	0 3 : 0 0	3 . p m	=	1 5 : 0 0
4 . a m	=	0 4 : 0 0	4 . p m	=	1 6 : 0 0
5 . a m	=	0 5 : 0 0	5 . p m	=	1 7 : 0 0
6 . a m	=	0 6 : 0 0	6 . p m	=	1 8 : 0 0
7 . a m	=	0 7 : 0 0	7 . p m	=	1 9 : 0 0
8 . a m	=	0 8 : 0 0	8 . p m	=	2 0 : 0 0
9 . a m	=	0 9 : 0 0	9 . p m	=	2 1 : 0 0
1 0 . a m	=	1 0 : 0 0	1 0 . p m	=	2 2 : 0 0
1 1 . a m	=	1 1 : 0 0	1 1 . p m	=	2 3 : 0 0

As you will know, at certain points during the year, our daily clocks go forward and backward 1 hour. During the winter we are in what is called Greenwich Mean Time, and during the summer we are in British Summer Time. To keep things simple, airlines and the Civil Aviation Authority always use GMT. This means that if we are currently in BST and on your roster you have to report for duty at 17:00, in real time terms you have to report at 18:00 as GMT is 1 hour behind BST. Admittedly at this stage it all sounds confusing, but the more you practise reading your times on a 24-hour clock and in GMT the easier it becomes.

Looking at the following table you can see what you might expect to see on your roster –

NAME	1st July	2nd July	3rd July	4th July	5th July	6th July	7th July
I. Smith	MAN - TFS MAN	Day Off	LGW - HER MAN	MAN - PMI MAN	Stand-by	Stand-by	LHR - IBZ MAN
	07:00 to 18:00		06:30 to 16:40	15:00 to 01:50	12:00 to 18:00	10:00 to 16:00	18:00 to 04:20

Lets look at July 1st. The roster says that you are flying to TFS, which is where? That's right, Tenerife South. So the flight departs 07:00 and returns back into Manchester at 18:00 GMT, meaning that as we are in BST the flight leaves at 08:00 and returns at 19:00.

On Friday July 7th you will see that this is no ordinary flight as it leaves London Heathrow and returns from its destination into Manchester. This is not an unusual occurrence if the airline you are working for has flights leaving more than one UK airport. For this particular flight you will have to 'reposition' which will involve being transported from your 'base' to London Heathrow. On this occasion you and the rest of the crew may be fortunate enough to be flown down to Heathrow or you may have to travel by coach or mini bus – it all depends on the airline. Looking back at the roster where is the flight going to and what are its estimated time of departure (e.t.d.) and estimated time of arrival (e.t.a.) in 'real times' – that is BST?

The flight you have been assigned for July 7th is going to Palma, Majorca. Its estimated time of departure in 'real time' is 19:00 and its estimated time of arrival is 05:20.

On this particular roster you have also been assigned 2 stand-by days. This means that between the hours given on the roster you should be contactable at all times and be prepared to be at base within 1 hour.

Now, try and work out what times the rest of the flights are in BST, and using the information from the relevant chapter, where the flights are to and from. Something not too dissimilar to this may come up during your first interview, so as always make sure you prepare well.

TEST

SECTION

<u>ADDITION PROBLEMS</u>

1)	3+7+12	26)	4325+765+876
2)	8+1+9	27)	1234+12+615
3)	6+5+11	28)	9878+7876+324
4)	13+5+9	29)	435+7874+231
5)	22+8+6	30)	1111+1111+2345
6)	43+11+19	31)	1234+5678+9876
7)	52+9+23	32)	1324+2435+3546
8)	11+3+36	33)	9983+2345+9812
9)	28+7+9	34)	2561+5837+9739
10)	333+98+3	35)	2341+9876+9872
11)	657+76+24	37)	2345+7563+9814
12)	553+12+91	37)	7364+8698+7641
13)	8+211+90	38)	9807+4356+5345
14)	87+999+12	39)	2342+7673+4321
15)	354+253+935	40)	3+98768+767+21
16)	12+11+877	41)	43+654+99999
17)	230+83+914	42)	345+12+43+9837+3
18)	34+66+475	43)	543+4532+32+4+53
19)	132+11+87	44)	544+9654+6543+99+54
20)	6454+12+987	45)	26+3245+33+52+42
21)	5467+7462+77	46)	342+2345+543+23+65
22)	5263+143+867	47)	543+34+43+654+443
23)	7864+6452+124	48)	654+22+654+56
24)	32+7657+231	49)	74+345+6546+3452+23
25)	6546+767+329	50)	765+8657+654+345+21

34

SUBTRACTION PROBLEMS

1)	21 - 13	26)	1234 - 987
2)	87 - 65	27)	9876 - 123
3)	99 - 54	28)	7464 - 534
4)	32 - 8	29)	8575 - 42
5)	55 - 7	30)	8842 - 1842
6)	39 - 11	31)	5325 - 2342
7)	66 - 24	32)	1231 - 421
8)	43 - 14	33)	7657 - 2621
9)	54 - 45	34)	7463 - 2347
10)	87 - 32	35)	5632 - 754
11)	762 - 432	36)	2546 - 875
12)	876 - 834	37)	8765 - 3453
13)	231 - 179	38)	4536 - 4367
14)	777 - 423	39)	7547 - 6435
15)	654 - 123	40)	82347 - 62435
16)	888 - 234	41)	63243 - 23542
17)	734 - 321	42)	64532 - 7544
18)	345 - 312	43)	87644 - 35226
19)	444 - 123	44)	75633 - 23562
20)	543 - 132	45)	75765 - 42563
21)	998 - 534	46)	76655 - 65367
22)	697 - 213	47)	88888 - 79999
23)	513 - 275	48)	345465 - 294565
24)	812 - 753	49)	765373 - 345264
25)	913 - 746	50)	986879 - 834576

MULTIPLICATION PROBLEMS

1)	12 x 6	26)	5433 x 9
2)	13 x 4	27)	7654 x 3
3)	64 x 8	28)	1234 x 8
4)	54 x 3	29)	6543 x 7
5)	23 x 7	30)	9112 x 6
6)	23 x 8	31)	12 x 13
7)	66 x 9	32)	43 x 12
8)	45 x 3	33)	44 x 17
9)	12 x 9	34)	54 x 15
10)	123 x 3	35)	33 x 20
11)	435 x 8	37)	11 x 16
12)	987 x 5	37)	65 x 14
13)	234 x 2	38)	99 x 11
14)	432 x 9	39)	78 x 43
15)	456 x 7	40)	641 x 24
16)	666 x 8	41)	645 x 81
17)	212 x 9	42)	733 x 89
18)	987 x 7	43)	912 x 32
19)	776 x 4	44)	123 x 87
20)	1111 x 3	45)	543 x 56
21)	2341 x 8	46)	5432 x 23
22)	6432 x 7	47)	6534 x 87
23)	9538 x 5	48)	1424 x 99
24)	6278 x 3	49)	2341 x 44
25)	4545 x 6	50)	5342 x 52

DIVISION PROBLEMS

1)	66 div by 6	26)	345 div by 5
2)	65 div by 5	27)	888 div by 3
3)	80 div by 4	28)	253 div by 9
4)	88 div by 2	29)	645 div by 6
5)	76 div by 6	30)	868 div by 8
6)	48 div by 4	31)	311 div by 7
7)	69 div by 3	32)	997 div by 4
8)	98 div by 6	33)	225 div by 9
9)	72 div by 4	34)	555 div by 6
10)	50 div by 5	35)	434 div by 5
11)	100 div by 4	36)	776 div by 8
12)	32 div by 8	37)	987 div by 2
13)	49 div by 7	38)	1234 div by 5
14)	72 div by 8	39)	2345 div by 4
15)	90 div by 5	40)	3456 div by 6
16)	123 div by 9	41)	4567 div by 7
17)	87 div by 7	42)	5678 div by 8
18)	221 div by 8	43)	6789 div by 9
19)	364 div by 3	44)	4321 div by 2
20)	65 div by 9	45)	5432 div by 3
21)	987 div by 6	46)	6543 div by 4
22)	99 div by 4	47)	7654 div by 5
23)	765 div by 2	48)	8765 div by 10
24)	546 div by 8	49)	1432 div by 11
25)	87 div by 9	50)	7436 div by 12

CURRENCY PROBLEMS

1) £GB1.00 is equal to 200 Spanish Pesetas.
   What is £GB10.00 worth in Spanish Pesetas?

2) £GB1.00 is worth $US1.50.
   What is £GB15.00 worth is $US?

3) £GB1.00 is worth 4000 Italian Lire.
   What is £GB30.00 worth in Italian Lire?

4) £GB1.00 is worth 12 French Francs.
   What is £GB5.00 worth in French Francs?

5) £GB1.00 is worth 3 Irish Punts.
   What is £GB9.00 worth in Irish Punts?

6) £GB1.00 is worth 175 Spanish Pesetas.
   What is £GB123.00 worth in Spanish Pesetas?

7) DM1.00 is worth $US6.00
   What is DM15.00 worth in $US?

8) 1 French Franc is worth $US3.00
   What is $US50.00 worth in French Francs?

9) 1 Swedish Kroner is worth DM1.08
   What is 50 Swedish Kroner worth in DM?

10) If a passenger wishes to pay in Portuguese Escudos, how much does he have to give you for goods up to the value of £GB8.00, presuming that there are 248 Escudo's to £GB1.00?

11) You are required to take £GB15.00 for a perfume and the passenger wishes to pay in Spanish Pesetas. Assuming that there are 180 Spanish Pesetas to £GB1.00, how many Spanish Pesetas does the passenger have to give you?

12) You are required to take £27.00 from a passenger for some drinks. He gives you 120,000 Italian Lire and requests his change in £GB. How much change will you give assuming that 5000 lire is equal to £GB2.00?

13) A passenger buys gifts worth £GB5.00, £GB2.50 and £GB33.99. They offer to pay in French Francs. If £GB1.00 is worth 9 French Francs how many French Francs will they have to give you?

COUNTRIES, CAPITALS AND CURRENCIES TEST

Below is a table with Countries, their capitals and their currencies. Now, from studying the country, capital and currency information in the Country Information chapter, can you remember what goes into the blanks without any help?

COUNTRY	CAPITAL	CURRENCY
Germany		Deutschmark
Finland	Helsinki	
	Edinburgh	
Australia		Aus. Dollar
	Wellington	
Japan		Japanese Yen
The Netherlands		Dutch Kroner
	Lisbon	Escudo
USA		US Dollar
Egypt	Cairo	
Spain		
		Drachma
	Ankara	
Wales	Cardiff	
		Schilling
Sweden		Swedish Kroner
	Copenhagen	
Ireland	Dublin	
		Belgian Franc
	Larnaca	
France		
	Bern	

Now check your answers with the 'Country Information' chapter. Once you have got the hang of getting the above 'blanks', get somebody to test you on all the other countries that you have information on.

GENERAL KNOWLEDGE

To help you with your General Knowledge skills I have compiled a list of questions that may possibly come up in one of the tests.

1. Who is the current Prime Minister of Great Britain?
2. On which continent is the Amazon?
3. What is the name of the world's highest mountain?
4. Name 3 languages spoken in Switzerland.
5. Who wrote the 'Famous Five' series of books?
6. Which political party is currently in power in the UK?
7. How many days are there in a year?
8. What does BBC stand for?
9. Which mountain range separates Spain from France?
10. Who is the president of the USA?
11. Who discovered Australia?
12. In which county is Norwich?
13. Name the orbital motorway around London.
14. What do GMT and BST stand for?
15. What is the time difference between the UK and Belgium?
16. Which is the largest continent?
17. Who wrote Oliver Twist?
18. Which river separates Wales from southern England?
19. Who was the first person to fly the English Channel?
20. Who was the first woman Prime Minister of England?
21. Name the Queen's eldest grandson.
22. Name the national airline of the UK?
23. Which is the largest lake in England?
24. Who is the current Education minister?
25. What is celebrated on July 4th in the USA?
26. Which body of water separates Europe from the USA?
27. Which is further South, Malta or Tunisia?
28. Which group of islands lie off the east coast of Spain?
29. Which country is the largest island in the world?
30. What is the national emblem of New Zealand?
31. What does EU stand for?
32. True or false. TAP is the national airline of Portugal?
33. Name 3 charter airlines.
34. Name 3 scheduled airlines.
35. What is the difference between charter and scheduled?
36. Name 3 makes of aircraft.
37. Name 3 aircraft model types.
38. Which is the world's busiest airport?
39. How many cigarettes can you bring back from a non-EU country?

40.   Which is the largest country in Europe (land area)?
41.   How many states make up the USA?
42.   True or false. Greenland is a part of Denmark?
43.   Where were the 2000 Olympic games held?
44.   What is the national emblem of Canada?
45.   Who owns Microsoft?
46.   Newark and JFK are airports in which US city?
47.   In which country is Schipol Airport?
48.   In what year did the Berlin Wall come down?
49.   The Apennines run down the centre of which country?
50.   Which mountain range runs down the eastern side of South America?
51.   Which four countries make up Scandinavia?
52.   In which country might Flemish be spoke?
53.   Which people are native to Australia?
54.   What does QANTAS stand for?
55.   On a flight from Manchester to Majorca, which bodies of water and mountain ranges are you likely to fly over?
56.   Pristina is in which country?
57.   What does CAA stand for?
58.   On what continent are the Himalayas?
59.   What is the fastest passenger aircraft in current use?
60.   Which four islands make up the Canary Islands?
61.   In aviation terms, what do the letters ETA and ETD stand for?
62.   Which company makes the A3XX range of planes?
63.   Which company makes the 747 aircraft?
64.   Who are the current World Cup holders in football?
65.   Name all of London's associated airports.
66.   To which country are the Falkland Islands closest?
67.   Which Roman built a wall to separate Scotland from England?
68.   What nationality is the Roman Catholic Pope?
69.   Which city do the 'Beatles' originate from?
70.   Which country is famous for producing Parma Ham?

The answers to these questions can be found in the 'Test Answers' section. Admittedly, the majority of these questions won't come up during the test section of your interview, but a few might and knowing the answers may be the difference between getting the job or a letter of rejection.

THE INTERVIEWS

By the time your first interview comes around you should have studied all the relevant chapters on how to prepare to a point where you are feeling really positive. I really can't stress how important it is to prepare for any interview. The more you know at this stage about what to expect can make a tremendous difference not only to your chances of getting the job you desire, but also your confidence levels going into the interview. I know that I am always less nervous going into a situation where I know what to expect due to thorough preparation, so make sure you can say the same.

The interview stage is where the airline will see you for the first time, so first impressions count. Make sure you are dressed impeccably and turn up on time! If it is possible travel to the interview site a couple of days before the interview so that you can time how long it takes to get there. This will hopefully mean that on the day of interview you can be confident that even if you are held up in traffic jams you will arrive on time. Dress code can be described as smart business wear. Men, wear a suit and tie, and ladies wear a knee length skirt with blouse and jacket. This sounds really obvious, but I've seen people blow their chances completely by turning up in Jeans and a sweatshirt.

The first interview is a group session and can last a couple of hours, but when the adrenaline is flowing the time passes really quickly. As you'll now know, it is at this point where you'll get tested on various topics and asked to display your presentation skills. There is also a lot more to it than this though, for it is here that you have to be aware that you are being monitored on how you interact with people. From the minute you walk in the door you have to be on your best behaviour, be polite, be friendly and most importantly be happy! The best way to go about this is to walk in confident and relaxed. Use all your social skills to introduce yourself to others and remember it is important that you listen to what other people have to say.

Once the session begins you must pay attention to all that is said as this may come up in the general knowledge test. If it's possible make notes at this stage to help you later. Throughout the session you will be interviewed, tested and asked to take part in a group discussion. When you are interviewed on a one to one basis be relaxed. More often than not the interviewer just wants to know a little bit more about you, such as where you live, what your interests are, why you want to do the job. Where appropriate recall what you have prepared in your self-presentation speech. If a question comes up that was also on the application form make sure that you answer it the same, they will have read it before the interview began. To help you remember what you wrote, make yourself a copy of the application form before you send it off and take it to the interview with you so that you can read it on the train or in the car park before you go in. For all other questions just answer them honestly, don't try to be too clever as they will be able to see right through you, honesty really is the best option! At this stage you may also be asked to present your exam certificates, record of achievement and driving licence, so have them prepared and present them neatly in a file so that the interviewer doesn't have to sift through pages of loose paper. Fail to prepare and prepare to fail again is the motto again! The discussion is used to see how you interact as a team member when you have a certain topic or problem to sort out. Although the subject matter will vary, the employers are looking to see whether you are too loud, too shy, too bossy etc.

Fortunately there is a happy medium which is relatively easy to fit into. Just be reasonable, confident and open to different opinions. More than likely you will be asked if you have any questions that you would like to ask. Be sensible, don't try to be too clever. I always find questions regarding promotion within the airline and what the airlines expansion plans are acceptable. For example, "What is the timescale between being appointed a cabin crew member and being able to apply for promotion to a cabin crew manager?, Does the airline plan to fly out of any different airports in the near future?, Does the airline plan to buy any new aircraft?". Try to avoid questions regarding money and benefits – usually these topics are covered either in the information that is sent to you with the application form or during the introduction.

The second interview can either take place straight after the first, or it may take place at a later date. If you make it this far you have done really well. Now it's just a case of putting the icing on the cake. The interview will probably last at least an hour and may be held by one or more interviewers. Its really difficult to say what you are going to be asked at this stage, but from my experience it is usually based along the lines of 'Why do you want to do the job?,' 'How will your past experience help you with this job?,' 'What would you do if........?'. Again, it is important to be prepared as much as possible, stay relaxed and answer as fully and clearly as you can. As in the first interview, they are not trying to catch you out with trick questions. Thinking logically before answering is always a good start. You won't be marked down for taking a couple of seconds to come up with a good answer, but you probably will be if you jump in straight away and get flustered half way through. Also, if you don't understand a question ask them to repeat it or explain what certain terminology means. Hopefully this book will help you understand most of the terms before you go in! The time will pass very quickly during the interview process and will be over before you know it. At the end, always try to thank the interviewer for giving you the interview and say that you hope to hear from them soon. The impression you give of yourself as you walk away at the end of the interview will probably last in their minds, so make sure it is a good one.

Some airlines may ask you to return for a third interview. This should be approached in the same way as the others – preparation is vital and is the key to success.

It is impossible to say exactly how soon after the final interview you will be told as to whether or not you have got the job. If you are getting this far and are then

43

being turned down, don't be despondent. Ask yourself where you are going wrong and try to remedy your errors. It may help to practise your interviewing style with a family member or friend, as they may be able to see more clearly where you need correcting. Just don't give up!

AIRLINE

DETAILS

AER LINGUS

- **Airline Type:** 'Scheduled'.
- **Year of Formation:** 1936
- **Company Colours:** Green and White

- **Airline Code:** EI
- **Base:** Dublin Airport
- **Departure Points (Ireland):** Dublin, Cork, Shannon, Belfast, Galway and Kerry

- **Fleet Models Include:**
  Airbus A320
  Airbus A321
  Airbus A330
  Boeing 737
  Boeing 767

- **Main Routes Include:** Amsterdam, Boston, Brussels, Chicago, Frankfurt, Leeds/Bradford, London Heathrow, Los Angeles, Manchester, Milan, New York, Paris,

- **Employees:** 5900

- **Recruitment Address:**
  Aer Lingus Ltd
  Cabin Crew Recruitment
  PO Box 180
  Dublin Airport
  Dublin
  Eire

- **Tel:** Republic of Ireland 1 886 2351
- **E-mail:** cabincrew@aerlingus.ie
- **Internet Address:** http://www.aerlingus.ie

Other Information

The name Aer Lingus is an anglicization of *Aer Loingeas*, the Irish for Air Fleet.
Air Lingus' first flight took place on the 27th May 1936 and was between Dublin and Bristol, UK.
Today Aer Lingus operates one of the youngest fleets of any European airline and have a 'dedicated staff committed to providing an excellent service, hoping to build on their impressive history'.

AIR 2000

- **Airline Type:** Mainly 'Charter', but 'Scheduled' routes to Paphos and Larnaca.
- **Date of Formation:** 11th April 1987
- **Owners:** First Choice Plc
- **Company Colours:** Various. A 'tapestry' theme reflecting the destinations to which the airline flys.

- **Airline Code:** AMM
- **Base:** Manchester International Airport
- **UK Departure Airports:** London Gatwick, Birmingham, Bristol, Manchester, Dublin, Belfast, Newcastle, Glasgow and Stansted airports.

- **Fleet Models Include:**
  Boeing 757
  Boeing 767
  Airbus A320
  Airbus A321

- **Main Routes Include:** Over 50 routes to the Mediterranean and various worldwide destinations including Orlando, Kenya, Mexico, Cyprus and the Caribbean.

- **Recruitment Address:**
  Air 2000 ltd
  Recruitment Department
  7th Floor, Commonwealth House
  Chicago Avenue
  Manchester Airport
  M90 3DP

- **Phone:** 0161 489 0327
- **Internet Address:** http://www.air2000.com

Other Information.

Air 2000 operates over 30,000 flights carrying 5 million passengers per year.
Air 2000 has won the Golden Globe Award for "Best UK Charter Airline" six times since the awards inception in 1990.
Company motto - "We don't carry businessmen to business meetings - we fly adventurers and sun seekers to exciting destinations around the world".

AIR CANADA

- **Airline Type:** 'Scheduled'.
- **Year of Formation:** 1937
- **Company Colours:** White, Red and Black

- **Airline Code:** AC
- **Base:** Montreal/Toronto

- **Fleet Models Include:**
  Airbus A319
  Airbus A320
  Airbus A330
  Airbus A340
  Boeing 747
  Boeing 767
  Canadair RJ100
  McDonnell Douglas DC-9

- **Main Routes Include:** Atlanta (GA), Antigua, Barbados, Boston (MA), Calgary (AB), Chicago (IL), New Delhi, Frankfurt, Glasgow, Hong Kong, Honolulu (HI), Manchester, Osaka, Paris, Quebec (PQ), San Francisco (CA), Seattle (WA), Toronto, Vancouver.

- **Employees:** 18000

- **Recruitment Address:**
  Air Canada Centre
  Cabin Crew Recruitment
  Zip 264
  PO Box 14 000
  Dorval (Quebec)
  H4Y 1H4
  Canada

- **Tel:** Canada 514 422 5000
- **Fax:** Canada 514 422 5650
- **Internet Address:** http://www.aircanada.ca

Other Information

Air Canada is a Canadian $4.9 billion operation that maintains a fleet of approximately 157 aircraft and serves over 545 destinations around the world. These statistics mean that Air Canada is the nations largest airline.

AIRTOURS

- **Airline Type:** 'Charter'.
- **Date of Formation:** 1980 as Pendle Air Tours
- **Company Chairman:** David Crossland
- **Company Colours:** White and Blue.

- **Airline Code:** AIH
- **Base:** Manchester International Airport
- **UK Departure Airports:** Birmingham, Bristol, Cardiff, Glasgow, London Gatwick Manchester, Newcastle, and Stansted airports.

- **Fleet Models Include:**
  Airbus A320
  Airbus A321
  Airbus A330
  Boeing 757
  Boeing 767

- **Main Routes Include:** Algarve, Austria, Barbados, Canada, Costa Blanca, Costa Del Sol, Cyprus, Dominican Republic, Florida, Gran Canaria, Italy, Majorca, Maldives, Rhodes, Tenerife, Thassos, Tunisia and Venice.

- **Recruitment Address:**
  Airtours International Plc
  Recruitment Department
  Parkway Three
  300 Princess Road
  Manchester
  M14 7QU

- **Internet Address:** http://www.airtours.co.uk

Other Information.

Airtous carry approximately 8 million passengers a year to over 65 destinations.
Airtours encompasses many other business interests and together they form the UK Leisure Group. Businesses included within this group include Panorama Holidays, Direct Holidays, Bridge Travel Group, Cresta Holidays, Tradewinds, Eurosites, JetSet, Going Places and Travelworld. The UK Leisure Group reported a year end (30th September 1999) total turnover of £1838.30 million.

Airtours' Aviation Division consists of the aviation interests of Airtous Plc. Brand names include Premiair (Scandinavia) and Air Belgium.

BRITANNIA

- **Airline Type:** 'Charter'.
- **Year of Formation:** 1962 under the name 'Euravia'. First flight was from Manchester to Majorca in May of that year.
- **Founder:** Ted Langton
- **Owners:** Thomson Corporation (Since 1965)
- **Company Colours:** Blue and White

- **Airline Code:** BY
- **Base:** London Luton Airport. The Britannia 757/767 hangar at Luton is larger than the dimensions of a football pitch and cost £10 million to build.
- **UK Departure Airports:** 17 airports in the UK including London Gatwick, Birmingham, Bristol, Manchester, Belfast, Newcastle, Glasgow and Stansted airports.

- **Fleet Models Include:**

  All Britannia aircraft are manufactured by the American manufacturer Boeing.

UK Based:	Germany Based:	Nordic Based:
757-204	767-304	737
767-204		757
767-304		

  Some of the fleet based in the UK are named. Below is a list of the people who have had aircraft named after them.

  Bobby Moore OBE, Roy Castle OBE, Bill Travers, Capt. Sir Ross Smith, Lord Horatio Nelson, Eglantyne Jebb-Founder of the Save the Children Fund, Sir Matt Busby CBE, Brian Johnston CBE MC, Eric Morecambe OBE.

- **Main Routes:** Over 100 destinations throughout the world, including 7 destinations in Australia during the Winter.

- **Recruitment Address:**
  Britannia Airways
  Recruitment & Training Centre
  East Midlands Airport
  Castle Donington
  Derby
  DE74 2SA

- **Internet Address:** http:// www.britanniaairways.com

50

Other Information.

Britannia is now Britain's second largest airline and is the worlds' biggest charter airline carrying approximately 8 million passengers a year. Britannia's fleet of Boeing aircraft travel over 54 million miles per year, equivalent to 2,000 times around the earth. Britannia doesn't just transport holidaymakers, but also carries over 3 million kilos of cargo per year, including fresh flowers, vegetables, computers and potato crisps.

Originally known as Euravia, Britannia was renamed Britannia Airways in 1964 as it began to replace the Lockheed Constellation aircraft with more modern Bristol 'Britannia' turboprop aircraft. Always the innovator, Britannia was the first airline to offer its holiday passengers hot meals. Another first was assigned seating. In 1968 Britannia entered the jet age to become the first European operator of the Boeing 737-200. In 1984, Britannia became the first UK holiday airline to offer passengers free in-flight audio and video entertainment. In 1988 the airline pioneered charter flights from the UK to Australia, and the following year to New Zealand. The 1990s have seen Britannia modernise its fleet and further expansion of their route network with the introduction of services to holiday destinations in Asia, South Africa and America. Long haul flying now accounts for some 30% of the airline's flying.

In 1997 Britannia formed a subsidiary company based in Germany to operate holiday flights for German tour operators. The airline, known as Britannia Airways GmbH, operates long haul and short haul flights from airports in Germany, Switzerland and Austria. 1998 saw the acquisition of the Scandinavian holiday operation, Fritidsresor Group, by the Thomson Travel Group, with Britannia acquiring the group's holiday airline, Blue Scandinavia, now known as Britannia AB. With bases at 4 airports in Sweden and Norway and some five hundred staff, Britannia AB is the second largest holiday airline in Scandinavia

Since 1995, Britannia has been involved with the Born Free Foundation. The airline has carried 9 big cats and raised over £310,000 for projects to help chimpanzees in Uganda, otters in Scotland and the current project, elephants in Kenya.

BRITISH AIRWAYS

- **Airline Type:** 'Scheduled'
- **Date of Formation:** 1919 as the Air Transport and Travel Company. First flight was from London to Paris in a DH4A Bomber, carrying a single passenger and a crate of letters.
- **Chairman (non-executive):** Lord Marshall of Knightsbridge
- **Company Colours:** White and Blue.

- **Airline Code:** BA
- **Base:** London Heathrow
- **UK Departure Airports:** London Gatwick, London Heathrow, Birmingham, Manchester, Newcastle, and Glasgow airports.

- **Fleet Models Include:**
  Airbus A320
  Boeing 737-200/300/400
  Boeing 747-100/200/400
  Boeing 757-200
  Boeing 767
  Boeing 777
  Concorde
  McDonnell Douglas DC-10

- **Main Routes Include:** 170 destinations in 70 countries in Europe, the Near, Middle and Far East, the Caribbean and the Americas. The domestic operations link 15 points in the UK and include 'super shuttle' services between London (Heathrow) and Glasgow, Edinburgh, Manchester and Belfast.

- **Recruitment Address:**
  British Airways
  Recruitment Department
  Meadowbank
  PO Box 59
  Hounslow
  TW5 9QX

- **Internet Address:** http://www.british-airways.com

Other Information.

14,864 (+ 218 support) cabin crew and 3285 Pilots and Co-Pilots
58,210 Total Employees (1996/7) 82% based in the UK.

£1855 million (aggregate payroll costs of employees).
38.2 million passengers during 1996/7 with an average of over 1000 flights a day.
721,000 tonnes of freight and mail carried.
Fleet comprises over 300 aircraft.

The company is owned totally by Private investors with 235,000 shareholders (87% are company employees).

British Airways has formed a 'Global Alliance' which includes the following airlines: QANTAS, Canadian Airlines, Air Liberte, TAT, Finnair and LOT Polish Airlines. The British Airways' global alliance, at March 31 1997 covered some 474 scheduled destinations in 103 countries.

Company Mission: "To be the undisputed leader in world travel" and also changed its corporate Goals and Values. The new Goals are to be the "Customers' Choice", to have "Inspired People", "Strong Profitability" and to be "Truly Global". The new values are to be "Safe and Secure", "Honest and Responsible", "Innovative and Team Spirited", "Global and Caring", and a "Good Neighbour".

BRITISH MIDLAND

- **Airline Type:** 'Scheduled'.
- **Year of Formation:** 1939 as 'Air Schools Limited'
- **Owners:** British Midland are a Plc. with Lufthansa and SAS being shareholders. Each has a 20% shareholding.
- **Company Colours:** Blue and Red

- **Airline Code:** BM
- **Base:** East Midlands Airport
- **UK Departure Airports:** Aberdeen, Belfast, Birmingham, Dublin, East Midlands, Edinburgh, Guernsey, Jersey, Leeds/Bradford, London Heathrow, Manchester, Teeside.

- **Fleet Models Include:**
  Airbus A320
  Airbus A321
  Boeing 737
  Embraer EMB-145
  Fokker 70
  Fokker 100

- **Main Routes Include:** Flights to all UK airports named above plus Amsterdam, Brussels, Budapest, Cologne, Copenhagen, Dresden, Dusseldorf, Esbjerg, Faro, Hanover, Malaga, Nice, Palma, Paris, Prague, Stuttgart, Warsaw.

- **Recruitment Address:**
  Personnel Department (Cabin Crew Recruitment)
  British Midland
  Donington Hall
  Castle Donington
  Derby
  East Midlands
  DE74 2SB

- **Internet Address:** http://www.iflybritishmidland.com

Other Information.

The British Midland motto is 'The Airline for Europe' Currently operating flights to over 30 European destinations and carrying over six million passengers per year British Midland is London Heathrow's second largest UK operator.

The company began operations in 1938 as Air Schools Ltd at Burnaston in Derby, specialising in flying instruction for RAF pilots, but in 1953 this was ceased. After World War 2, Air Schools Ltd diversified to form Derby Aviation and offered ad-hoc passenger and cargo charters, maintenance and aircraft brokerage. The first international route operated by Derby Aviation was to Ostend from the company's base at Burnaston in 1953. Derby Aviation changed its name to Derby Airways in 1959 and began operating inclusive tour holidays abroad. The scheduled route network expanded to include 15 UK cities.

Another name change occurred in 1964 when Derby Airways, a UK pioneer in the package holiday industry and became British Midland Airways (BMA). By 1970 BMA was a key player, operating charter flights to the USA and other long-haul destinations. 1972 saw British Midland Airways make a dramatic decision. The airline withdrew from the holiday tour market and the fleet was consolidated to become an 'instant airline' which provided fully liveried aircraft, with crew and ground staff to countries wanting to operate their own fledgling national airlines. The 'instant airline' concept proved so successful the airline was awarded the Queens Award to industry for its export achievements.

The launch of the first trunk route in 1982 between London Heathrow and Glasgow meant lower fares and in-flight service benefits. This was followed in 1983 with a service from Heathrow to Edinburgh. BMA was also voted Best Domestic Airline by Executive Travel magazine for the first time.

With the launch of Diamond EuroClass in 1993, British Midland became the first European airline to offer a separate business class cabin to Europe's business travellers with a range of business class fares offering savings of up to 40% and all the business class privileges.

As part of its on-going arrangement with the German national airline, Lufthansa, British Midland has introduced code-share flights from Manchester to Dusseldorf. Deutsche Lufthansa AG ('Lufthansa') has a 20 per cent stake in the company. The shares being acquired from Scandinavian Airlines System whose stake in BM has therefore reduced to 20 per cent from the 40 per cent held since 1992. The sale was conditional on BM's entry into Star Alliance and necessary regulatory consent.

LEARNING RESOURCES CENTRE
STAMFORD COLLEGE
DRIFT ROAD
STAMFORD PE9 1XA

EMIRATES

- **Airline Type:** 'Scheduled'.
- **Year of Formation:** 1985
- **Company Colours:** White and Red

- **Airline Code:** EK
- **Base:** Dubai, United Arab Emirates

- **Fleet Models Include:**
  Airbus A300
  Airbus A310
  Airbus A330
  Boeing 777

- **Main Routes Include:** Amman, Athens, Damascus, Delhi, Doha, Dubai, Frankfurt, Hong Kong, Islamabad, Istanbul, Jeddah, Kuala Lumpur, Larnaca, Manchester, Melbourne, Paris, Riyadh, Rome, Singapore, Stockholm, Tehran and Zurich

- **Employees:** 4000

- **Recruitment Address:**
  Emirates
  Cabin Crew Recruitment
  PO Box 686
  Dubai
  United Arab Emirates

  London applicants can contact Kay Lawrence via e-mail:
  kaylawrence@emirates.com

- **Internet Address:** http://www.ekgroup.com
- **Downloadable Application Form:**
  http://www.emiratesairline.com/employment/CrewAppForm.doc

Other Information

Since its creation in 1985, Emirates has won 190 awards for excellence.
Emirates' objectives are: "to offer the best service on every route it operates; to provide a link between the UAE's main trading partners; to develop new ones, capitalising on Dubai's pivotal geographic position and the infrastructure and service levels the Emirate offers as a regional business and distribution center"

EASYJET

- **Airline Type:** 'Scheduled'
- **Date of Formation:**
- **Owner:** Mr Stelios Haji-Ioannou
- **Company Colours:** Orange and White.

- **Airline Code:** EZY
- **Base:** London Luton Airport
- **UK Departure Airports:** London Luton, Liverpool.

- **Fleet Models Include:**
  Boeing 737's

- **Main Routes Include:** Aberdeen, Amsterdam, Athens, Barcelona, Belfast, Edinburgh, Geneva, London Gatwick, London Stansted, Madrid, Malaga, Nice, Palma, Zurich.

- **Recruitment Address:**
  easyJet Airline Company Limited
  Cabin Crew Recruitment
  easyLand
  London Luton Airport
  Bedfordshire LU2 9LS
  UK

- **Internet Address:** http://www.easyjet.com

Other Information.

Mission Statement: "To provide our customers with safe, low-cost, good value, point-to-point air services. To offer a consistent and reliable product at fares appealing to leisure and business markets from our bases to a range of domestic and European destinations. To achieve this we will develop our people and establish lasting partnerships with our suppliers".

IBERIA

- **Airline Type:** 'Scheduled'.
- **Year of Formation:** 28th June, 1927
- **Owners:** SEPI – 93.84% Employees – 6.14%
- **Company Colours:** White, Red and Orange

- **Airline Code:** IB
- **Base:** Madrid, Spain
- **Departure Airports Include:** Almeria, Arrecife, Barcelona, Granada, Ibiza, La Coruna, Madrid, Oviedo, Palma de Mallorca, Santander, Zaragoza.

- **Fleet Models Include:**
  Airbus A300
  Airbus A319
  Airbus A320
  Airbus A340
  Boeing 727 / 737 / 747 / 757 / 767
  McDonnell Douglas DC 8 / DC9/ / DC10
  McDonnell Douglas MD 87

- **Main Routes Include:**
- Athens, Barcelona, Belfast, Berlin, Brussels, Copenhagen, Dusseldorf, Helsinki, Larnaca, London, Manchester, Marseille, Milan, Porto, Zurich.

- **UK Address:**
  Iberia Airlines of Spain
  Venture House
  27-29 Glasshouse Street
  London
  W1R 6JU

- **Recruitment E-mail Address (UK)** - personnel@iberiaairlines.co.uk
- **Internet Address:** http://www.iberia.com

Other Information.

Employees: 29,079
Average number of flights daily: 920
Passengers carried in 1999: 26,344 million
First flight was between Madrid and Barcelona on June 14th 1927
Iberia are a partner in the oneworld alliance which includes American Airlines and British Airways.

JERSEY EUROPEAN

- **Airline Type:** 'Scheduled'.
- **Year of Formation:** 1979
- **Owners:** Walkersteel Group.
- **Company Colours:** White, red, orange and yellow.

- **Airline Code:** JE
- **Base:** Exeter Airport
- **UK Departure Airports:** Belfast, Birmingham, Blackpool, Bristol, Edinburgh, Exeter, Glasgow International, Guernsey, Isle of Man, Jersey, Leeds, London City, London Gatwick, London Heathrow, London Stansted, Southampton.

- **Fleet Models Include:**
  Bae 146 Whisper Jet (100/200/300 Series)
  Canadair Regional Jet (200 Series)
  Bombardier Dash 8 (Q 200/300/400 Series)
  Shorts SD360

- **Main Routes Include:** There are flights to and from all the UK departure airports plus flights to Cork, Dublin, Paris Charles de Gaulle, Shannon, Toulouse

- **Recruitment Address:**
  Personnel Department (Cabin Crew Recruitment)
  Jersey European
  Exeter Airport
  EX5 2BD
  United Kingdom

- **Tel:** 01392 366669 (Personnel Department)
- **Internet Address:** http://www.jerseyeuropean.co.uk

Other Information.

- Over 1000 flights a week
- Air France franchise services to Paris (CDG), Lyons and Toulouse
- No 1 carrier to and from Channel Islands and Northern Ireland
- 3rd largest scheduled airline at Birmingham International
- Turnover £152.9 million (year to end March 1999)
- Over 1300 staff

Board Members:
Barry Perrott – Chief Executive
Jim French – Deputy Chief Executive and Chief Operating Officer
Simon Chance – Chief Technical Officer
Stuart Carson – Chief Financial Officer
David Quick – Chief Officer Group Services

Jersey European was formed in 1979 from the merger of Jersey-based Intra Airways and Bournemouth-based Express Air Services. In 1983 the company was taken over by the Walkersteel group, already the parent company of Blackpool-based charter airline, Spacegrand.

Jersey European gained its first London route in 1991 from Guernsey to London Gatwick and shortly afterwards the route from Jersey to London Gatwick began operation.

Jersey European was recognised as a major regional airline when it won the 'Best UK Regional Airline' award for 1993 and 1994 at the Northern Ireland Travel and Tourism awards.

In 1996 the first franchise routes in conjunction with Air France began from London Heathrow to Toulouse and Lyons.

Change in appearance for Jersey European came about with the introduction of a new uniform which complemented the new corporate business image. The new Business Class upgrade included leather seats on all BAe 146 aircraft, advance seat selection, dedicated check-in and priority baggage handling. These features emphasise the Airline's continued commitment to business passengers.

Since its formation, Jersey European Airways has grown to become one of the UK's leading carriers with passenger figures now topping 2 million a year, developing a network to suit both business and leisure passengers.

KLM

- **Airline Type:** 'Scheduled'.
- **Year of Formation:** October 7th 1919
- **Chairman:** C.J. Oort
- **Company Colours:** White and Blue

- **Airline Code:** KL
- **Base:** Amsterdam Schipol
- **Departure Airports:** Amsterdam Schipol

- **Fleet Models Include:**
  Boeing 737
  Boeing 767
  Boeing 747
  Fokker50/70
  McDonnell-Douglas MD11
  SAAB 340B

- **Main Routes Include:**
  Detroit, London Stansted, Milan, Minneapolis, Nairobi, Oslo and Rome.

- **Downloadable Application Form:**
  http://jobs.klm.com/dcp/download/applicationForm.doc

- **Internet Address:** http://www.klm.com

Other Information:

KLM's first flight was between Amsterdam and London on May 17th 1920.
KLM carried 15,041 million passengers and 578,000 tons of cargo and mail in 1998/99.
KLM and its partner airlines operate a route network connecting more than 500 cities in 90 countries on 6 continents

KLM aims to:
- Offer a high-quality product at a competitive price
- Strengthen market presence, in part through alliances with other carriers
- Achieve internationally competitive cost levels, on a sound financial basis.

KLM's Mission Statement:
"KLM wants to excel in the quality of its connections, by linking as many cities as possible. KLM's goal is to participate in one of the leading global airline systems as an independent and financially strong European partner".

KLM UK

- **Airline Type:** 'Scheduled'.
- **Year of Formation:** February 1998 (Formerly Air UK founded 1980)
- **Owners:** KLM Royal Dutch Airlines (Majority shareholders)
- **Company Colours:** White and Blue

- **Airline Code:** UK
- **Base:** London Stansted
- **UK Departure Airports:** Aberdeen, Birmingham, Bristol, Cardiff, Edinburgh, Glasgow, Humberside, Leeds/Bradford, London City, London Heathrow, London Stansted, Manchester, Newcastle, Norwich, Teesside.

- **Fleet Models Include:**
  ATR72 202
  BAe 146 (100/300 series)
  F27 500
  Fokker 50 and 100's

- **Main Routes Include:**
  Amsterdam, Berlin Tegel, Brussells, Dusseldorf, Frankfurt, Milan (Malpensa), Paris (Charles de Gaulle), Rotterdam. In total, KLM UK offers over 1,600 scheduled flights a week to 30 destinations in the UK and Continental Europe.

- **Recruitment Address:**
  KLM UK
  Cabin Crew Recruitment
  Stansted House
  Stansted Airport
  Stansted
  Essex
  CM24 1AE

- **Tel:** 01279 660400
- **Internet Address:** http://www.airuk.co.uk

Other Information.

Air UK has been a wholly owned subsidiary of KLM Royal Dutch Airlines since July 1997. The relationship between the two carriers stretches back to the 1980s when the newly-formed Air UK was beginning to develop its network out of Britain. Air UK operated feeder services from UK regional airports into KLM's own homebase of Amsterdam Airport Schiphol.

LUFTHANSA

- **Airline Type:** 'Scheduled'.
- **Year of Formation:** 1926
- **Chairman:** Jurgen Weber
- **Company Colours:** White and Blue

- **Airline Code:** LH
- **Base:** Frankfurt/Main International.
- **Departure Airports Include:** Berlin, Dresden, Friedrichschafen, Hamburg, Hannover, Munich, Nuremberg.

- **Fleet Models Include:**
Airbus A300
Airbus A310
Airbus A319
Airbus A320
Airbus A321
Airbus A340
Boeing 737
Boeing 747

- **Main Routes Include:**
Abu Dhabi, Accra, Ankara, Athens, Bahrain International, Bangkok International, Barcelona, Belgrade, Birmingham (UK), Brussels, Chicago, Dubai, Edinburgh, Graz, Kiev,Lisbon, Malaga, San Francisco, Toronto.

- **Internet Address:** http://www.lufthansa.com

Other Information:

28,000 employees of which 9000 are flight attendants.
Lufthansa was the first airline to set up an airmail service across the South Atlantic.
1970 saw Lufthansa become the first European airline to commercially operate the Boeing 747.
In 1975, passengers carried totalled over 10 million for the first time.
In 1998, Lufthansa carried 40.5 million passengers.

MONARCH

- **Airline Type:** Mainly 'Charter', but some 'Scheduled' routes. Monarch is the principal provider of charter seats to the small to medium sized tour operators.
- **Date of Formation:** 1967. First flight Friday 5th April 1968 from Luton to Madrid.
- **Joint Managing Directors:** Mr Don McAngus and Mr Danny Bernstein
- **Company Colours:** Black and Yellow .
- **Staff:** 2400

- **Airline Code:** MON
- **Base:** London Luton Airport
- **UK Departure Airports:** London Luton, London Gatwick, Manchester International, Birmingham and Leeds Bradford.

- **Fleet Models Include:**
  Airbus A300-600R
  Airbus A320
  Airbus A330
  Boeing 757-200
  McDonnell Douglas DC-10

- **Main Routes Include:**
  Over 100 routes to the Mediterranean and various worldwide destinations. Carrying over 5 million passengers per year it is now the second largest charter airline in the UK.

- **Recruitment Address:**
  Monarch
  Recruitment Department
  London Luton Airport
  Luton
  LU2 9NU

- **Internet Address:** http://www.monarch-airlines.com

Other Information:

Monarch recognises the importance of a high standard of in-flight service. The cabin crew work as a small, efficient and, above all, friendly team. Each member undergoes a five-week training course before coming into contact with passengers. The uniform is updated every eighteen months and the distinctive black and yellow is easily recognisable.

QANTAS

- **Airline Type:** 'Scheduled'.
- **Year of Formation:** 1920
- **Chief Executive:** Mr James Strong
- **Company Colours:** White and Red

- **Airline Code:** QF
- **Base:** Sydney International Airport, Australia
- **UK Departure Airports:** London Heathrow.

- **Fleet Models Include:**
  Boeing 737's
  Boeing 747's
  Boeing 767's
  Qantas subsidiary regional airlines operate a mixed fleet of de Havilland, Shorts and British Aerospace aircraft.

- **Main Routes Include:**
  565 flights a day to 50 destinations in all Australian states and mainland territories.
  370 international flights every week from Australia, offering services to 54 destinations in 32 other countries.

- **Recruitment Address:**
  QANTAS
  Cabin Crew Recruitment
  203 Coward Street
  Mascot NSW 2020
  AUSTRALIA

- **Tel:** Australia 2 9691 3636
- **Internet Address:** http://www.qantas.com.au

Other Information.

QANTAS stands for the Queensland and Northern Territory Aerial Services.
Qantas is the world's second oldest airline. It was founded in the Queensland outback in 1920. Qantas is recognised as one of the world's leading long distance airlines, having pioneered services from Australia to North America and Europe. Qantas employs around 29,000 staff across a network which spans 104 destinations in Australia, Africa, the Americas, Asia, Europe, the Middle East and the Pacific.

SABENA

- **Airline Type:** Scheduled
- **Date of Formation:** 1919 (Under the name of SNETA – became Sabena in 1923)
- **Company Colours:** White and Blue .
- **Staff:** 10,698 (1694 Cabin Crew)

- **Airline Code:** SAB
- **Base:** Brussels, Belgium.
- **Departure Airports:** Brussels National Airport, Antwerp

- **Fleet Models Include:**
  Airbus A319
  Airbus A320
  Airbus A321
  Airbus A330
  Airbus A340
  Boeing 737
  Boeing 747

- **Recruitment Address:**
  Aéroport de Bruxelles National
  Bâtiment 201
  1820 Steenokkerzeel
  Brussels
  Belgium

- **Tel:** Belgium 02 723 76 41
- **Internet Address:** http://www.sabena.com

Other Information:

Sabena Mission: "To serve airline customers safely, punctually and profitably from the heart of Europa."
Sabena Vision: "We will grow worldwide as a sustained profitable airline Group by: exceeding cost effectively the needs of our customers, leveraging our partnerships and developing our people".

Sabena has alliances with other airlines including: Swissair, Austrian Airlines, Crossair, lauda Air, Tyrolean Airways, AOM, Air Littoral, Turkish Airlines, TAP Air Portugal, Air Europe.

SWISSAIR

- **Airline Type:** Scheduled
- **Date of Formation:** March 26th 1931
- **Company Colours:** White and Red.
- **Staff:** 7,678 (3449 cabin crew) at December 1998

- **Airline Code:** SW
- **Base:** Zurich, Switzerland
- **Departure Airports Include:** Basle, Geneva, Zurich
- **Main Routes Include:** Istanbul, Jeddah, Moscow, Nice, Nuremberg, Tel Aviv

- **Fleet Models Include:**
  Airbus A310
  Airbus A319
  Airbus A320
  Airbus A321
  Airbus A330
  Bae 146
  Boeing 747
  McDonnell Douglas DC 4
  McDonnell Douglas MD 11
  McDonnell Douglas MD 81

- **Recruitment Address:**
  Swissair, Human Resources Cabin Personnel PFKC
  8058 Zürich-Flughafen
  Zurich
  Switzerland

- **Tel:** Switzerland 01 812 56 46

- **Internet Address:** http://www.swissair.com

Other Information:

169,030 commercial flights were operated by Swissair in 1998
Annual revenue 1998 – CH F 5,119 million
Swissair has co-operation accords with many airlines including: Air Littoral, AOM, Austrian Airlines, Crossair, Lauda Air, Sabena, TAP Air Portugal, Turkish Airlines and Tyrolean Airways.

TWA

- **Airline Type:** Scheduled
- **Date of Formation:** July 13th, 1925 as Western Air Express. Changed name to Trans World Airlines in 1950.
- **Company Colours:** Blue, Red and White
- **Chairman:** Gerald Gitner
- **President:** Capt. William F. Compton
- **Staff:** 21,000

- **Airline Code:** TWA
- **Departure Airports Include:** St.Louis and New York (JFK) are the main hubs. Alberquerque, Anchorage, Baltimore, Boston, Cleveland, Detroit, Houston, Las Vegas, New York, San Francisco, Tampa, Washington

- **Fleet Models Include:**
Airbus A330
Boeing 727
Boeing 747
Boeing 757
Boeing 767
McDonnell Douglas DC 9
McDonnell Douglas MD 82
McDonnell Douglas MD 83
McDonnell Douglas MD 90

- **Routes:** 132 destinations, including 33 served by regional airline partners that operate as either Trans World Express or Trans World Connection, in 13 countries in North America, the Caribbean, Europe, Africa and the Middle East.

- **Recruitment Address:** (Send cover letter and resume)

Trans World Travel Academy
11495 Natural Bridge Road
Suite 416
St. Louis
MO 63044
United States of America

- **Tel:** United States (314) 589-3000
- **Fax:** United States (314) 895-6881

- **Internet Address:** http://www.twa.com
- **E-mail:** twa@twa.com

Other Information:

TWA'S revenue in 1998 was more than $US 3.2 billion, serving in excess of 25 million passengers.

TWA operates approximately 820 flights every day.
TWA's first intercontinental flight was between New York and Paris on February 5th 1946.

TWA received the 1999 J.D.Power & Associates/*Frequent Flyer* Magazine award as the Number 1 U.S. airline for customer satisfaction on flights of less than 500 miles.

TWA have been pioneers in the airline industry being the first to:
Fly coast-to-coast in the United States (on a route laid out by Charles Lindbergh).
First in the U.S. to operate a pressurized all-weather aircraft (the Boeing Stratoliner).
First to offer non-stop coast-to-coast service in the U.S.
First to brew fresh coffee in flight.
First to offer in-flight movies.
First to fly the Boeing 747 in the United States.
First to fly the Atlantic using twin-engine jet aircraft.

UNITED AIRLINES

- **Airline Type:** Scheduled
- **Date of Formation:** April 6th, 1926
- **Company Colours:** Gray, Navy and Red
- **Chairman and CEO:** Gerald Greenwald
- **President:** John Edwardson

- **Airline Code:** UA
- **Base:** Chicago O' Hare
- **Departure Airports Include:** Chicago, Los Angeles, Miami, Newark, Orlando, San Francisco, Washington

- **Fleet Models Include:**
  Airbus A319
  Airbus A320
  Boeing 727 / 737 / 747 / 757 / 767 / 777
  McDonnell Douglas DC 10

- **Main International Routes Include:**
  Auckland, Beijing, Brussels, Dusseldorf, Frankfurt, London, Melbourne, Munich, Paris, Singapore, Sydney

- **Recruitment Address:**
  Employment Office—WHQEJ
  P.O. Box 66100
  Chicago, IL 60666
  United States of America

- **Tel:** (USA) 1-888-UAL-JOBS (UK) 0845 8444 777

- **Internet Address:** http://www.ual.com

Other Information:

On May 15,1930, Boeing Air Transport, a United subsidiary, introduced the world's first stewardess service. Ellen Church, a former nurse, was one of the first stewardesses.

On Dec. 22, 1993, the UAL board approved a proposal for 54,000 employees to exchange portions of their salaries and benefits for UAL stock, paving the way for the creation on July 12, 1994, of the largest majority employee-owned company in the world.

VIRGIN ATLANTIC

- **Airline Type:** 'Scheduled' and 'Charter' in the guise of Virgin Express
- **Date of Formation:** 1984.
- **Owner:** Sir Richard Branson
- **Company Colours:** White and Red.

- **Airline Code:** VS
- **Base:** London Heathrow
- **UK Departure Airports:** London Gatwick, London Heathrow and Manchester International.

- **Fleet Models Include:**
  Airbus A320-200
  Airbus A340-300
  Boeing 747 Classics
  Boeing 747-400

- **Main Routes Include:**
  Athens, Cape Town, Chicago, Hong Kong, Los Angeles, Miami, New York (JFK), New York (Newark), Orlando, San Francisco, Singapore and Tokyo.

- **Recruitment Address:**
  Virgin Atlantic
  Recruitment Department (Cabin Crew)
  Heathrow Airport
  Heathrow
  Middlesex

- **Internet Address:** http://www.virgin-atlantic.com

Other Information.

The first flight was on the 22 June 1984 a plane packed with friends, celebrities and the media set off for Newark, New York – Virgin Atlantic was born.

Virgin Atlantic still holds to the founding principles of offering cut-price, long-haul air travel with some attendant stylishness. As Virgin's passenger figures have grown and as the airline has matured, its image has slowly evolved from that of a cheap-ticket transatlantic carrier to one that offers solid competition for the business traveller with its upper class service providing the bulk of its operating profit.

TEST

ANSWERS

SECTION

MATHS ANSWERS

Below and over the next couple of pages are the answers to the addition, subtraction, multiplication, division and currency problems that were set earlier on in the book. Make sure that you have double-checked that you believe your answers are correct before you check them against the answers below. If you find that you are getting some wrong, go back and see if it is a simple error such as writing down the sum incorrectly. It may be necessary for you to read through the relevant part of the chapter again to see where you are making your mistakes.

Addition Answers

1)	22	26)	5966
2)	18	27)	1861
3)	22	28)	18078
4)	27	29)	8540
5)	36	30)	4567
6)	73	31)	16788
7)	84	32)	7305
8)	50	33)	22140
9)	44	34)	18137
10)	434	35)	22089
11)	757	36)	19722
12)	656	37)	23703
13)	309	38)	19508
14)	1098	39)	14336
15)	1542	40)	99559
16)	900	41)	100696
17)	1227	42)	10240
18)	575	43)	5164
19)	230	44)	16894
20)	7453	45)	3398
21)	13006	46)	3318
22)	6273	47)	1717
23)	14440	48)	1386
24)	7920	49)	10440
25)	7642	50)	10442

So, how many did you get correct? You should be looking to get at least 90% correct which is 45 out of the 50 sums that were set. This standard should be carried throughout all of the tests that have been set for you to complete. Now lets check the rest of the problems that have been set for you to do.

Subtraction Answers

1)	8	26)	247
2)	22	27)	9753
3)	45	28)	6930
4)	24	29)	8533
5)	48	30)	7000
6)	28	31)	2983
7)	42	32)	810
8)	29	33)	5036
9)	9	34)	5116
10)	55	35)	4878
11)	330	36)	1671
12)	42	37)	5303
13)	52	38)	169
14)	354	39)	1112
15)	531	40)	19912
16)	654	41)	39701
17)	413	42)	56988
18)	33	43)	52418
19)	321	44)	52071
20)	411	45)	33202
21)	464	46)	11288
22)	484	47)	8889
23)	238	48)	50900
24)	59	49)	420109
25)	167	50)	152303

Multiplication Answers

1)	72	26)	48897
2)	52	27)	22962
3)	512	28)	9872
4)	162	29)	45801
5)	161	30)	54672
6)	184	31)	156
7)	594	32)	516
8)	135	33)	748
9)	108	34)	810
10)	369	35)	660
11)	3480	36)	176
12)	4935	37)	910
13)	468	38)	1089
14)	3888	39)	3354
15)	3192	40)	15384
16)	5328	41)	52245
17)	1908	42)	65237
18)	6909	43)	29184
19)	3104	44)	10701
20)	3333	45)	30408
21)	18728	46)	124936
22)	45024	47)	568458
23)	47690	48)	140976
24)	18834	49)	103004
25)	27270	50)	277784

Division Answers

1)	11.00	26)	69.00
2)	13.00	27)	296.00
3)	20.00	28)	28.11
4)	44.00	29)	107.50
5)	12.67	30)	108.50
6)	12.00	31)	44.43
7)	23.00	32)	249.25
8)	16.33	33)	25.00
9)	18.00	34)	92.50
10)	10.00	35)	86.80
11)	25.00	36)	97.00
12)	4.00	37)	493.50
13)	7.00	38)	246.80
14)	9.00	39)	586.25
15)	18.00	40)	576.00
16)	13.67	41)	652.43
17)	12.43	42)	709.75
18)	27.63	43)	754.33
19)	121.33	44)	2160.50
20)	7.22	45)	1810.67
21)	164.50	46)	1635.75
22)	24.75	47)	1530.80
23)	382.50	48)	876.50
24)	68.25	49)	130.18
25)	9.67	50)	619.67

Currency Answers

1)	2000 Spanish Pesetas	8)	16.67 French Francs
2)	$US 22.50	9)	DM 54
3)	120000 Italian Lire	10)	1984 Portuguese Escudos
4)	60 French Francs	11)	2700 Spanish Pesetas
5)	27 Irish Punts	12)	£GB 21.00
6)	21525 Spanish Pesetas	13)	373.41 French Francs
7)	$US 90.00		

GENERAL KNOWLEDGE
ANSWERS

1. Tony Blair
2. South America
3. Mount Everest
4. French, German and Italian
5. Enid Blyton
6. Labour
7. 365 (366 in a leap year)
8. British Broadcasting Corporation
9. The Pyranees
10. Bill Clinton
11. Captain James Cook
12. Norfolk
13. M25
14. Greenwich Mean Time and British Summer Time
15. + 1 hour
16. Asia
17. Charles Dickens
18. River Severn
19. Louis Bleriot
20. Margaret Thatcher
21. Peter Phillips
22. British Airways
23. Windermere
24. David Blunkett
25. Independence Day
26. Atlantic Ocean
27. Malta
28. Balearics
29. Australia
30. Kiwi
31. Economic Union
32. True
33. Charter – Airtours, Flying Colours, Britannia.
34. Scheduled – British Airways, Virgin, British Midland.
35. Charter fly 'holiday' routes and are part of a travel
    company ie. Britannia is owned by Thomson. Schedule airlines fly set
    routes and times and are independent,eg. Virgin, British Airways.
36. Eg. Boeing, Airbus, McDonnell-Douglas.
37. Eg. 737, 747, 757, A320, A321, Concorde.
38. Chicago O' Hare
39. 200
40. Russia

41. 50
42. True
43. Sydney, Australia
44. Maple Leaf
45. Bill Gates
46. New York
47. Netherlands
48. 1989
49. Italy
50. The Andes
51. Finland, Norway, Sweden and Denmark
52. Belgium
53. Aborigines
54. Queensland And Northern Territories Air Service
55. English Channel, Pyranees Mountains, Mediterranean Sea
56. Kosova
57. Civil Aviation Authority
58. Asia
59. Concorde
60. Tenerife, Gran Canaria, Lanzarote and Fuertaventura
61. Estimated Time of Arrival and Estimated Time of Departure
62. Airbus
63. Boeing
64. France
65. Heathrow, Gatwick, London City, London Stanstead and London Luton
66. Argentina
67. Hadrian
68. Polish
69. Liverpool
70. Italy

* At the time of going to press, all the answers to the above general knowledge questions were correct. We apologise if any of the answers have changed. They will be corrected for the next re-print.

USEFUL

ADDRESSES

AND

WEB

SITES

USEFUL ADDRESSES

BRITISH REGIONAL AIRWAYS
Cabin Crew Recruitment
Ronaldsway Airport
Ballasalla
Isle of Man
IM9 2JE

CALEDONIAN
Cabin Crew Recruitment
Caledonian House
Gatwick Airport
West Sussex
RH6 0LF

GO
Cabin Crew Recruitment
Enterprise House
Stansted Airport
Essex
CM24 1SB

AIR EUROPE
Cabin Crew Recruitment
Via Carlo Noe
3, 21013
Gallarate (VA)
Italy

CATHAY PACIFIC AIRWAYS
Cabin Crew Recruitment
Swire House
5th Floor
Connaught Street Central
Hong Kong SAR
China

LEISURE INTERNATIONAL
Personnel Department
Stansted House
Stansted Airport
Essex
CM24 1AE

SABRE AIRWAYS Ltd
12 The Merlin Centre
County Oak Way
Crawley
West Sussex
RH11 7XA

TRANSAER
Cabin Crew Recruitment
Transaer House
Dublin Airport
Dublin
Reoublic of Ireland

EL AL ISRAELI AIRLINES
Cabin Crew Recruitment
PO Box 41
Ben-Guiron Int'l Airport
Tel Aviv 70 100
Israel

INDIAN AIRLINES
Cabin Crew Recruitment
Airlines House
113 Gurdwara Rakabganj Road
New Delhi 110001
India

AIRLINE WEB SITES

European Airlines

A

AB Airlines	http://www.abairlines.com
Adria Airways	http://www.kabi.si/si21/aa
Aer Lingus	http://www.aerlingus.ie
Aero Lloyd	http://www.aerolloyd.de
Aeroflot	http://www.aeroflot.org
Aerosweet Airlines	http://www.aerosweet.com
Air 2000	http://www.air2000.com
Air Atlanta	http://www.atlanta.is
Air Baltic	http://www.airbaltic.lv
Air Berlin	http://www.airberlin.de
Air Dolomiti	http://www.airdolomiti.it/indexing.html
Air Engiadina	http://www.airengiadina.ch
Air Europa	http://www.air-europa.com
Air Europe	http://www.aireurope.it
Air France	http://www.airfrance.fr
Air Georgia	http://www.air-georgia.com
Air Lithuania	http://vingis.sc-uni.ktu.lt/airlit
Air Littoral	http://www.airlittoral.com
Air Malta	http://www.airmalta.com
Air Moldova	http://www.ami.md
Air One	http://www.air-one.it
Airtours	http://www.airtours.co.uk
Alitalia	http://www.alitalia.com
AOM French Airlines	http://www.aom.com
Aurigny Air	http://www.aurigny.com
Austrian Airlines	http://www.aua.com
Azzurra Air	http://www.azzurraair.it/eng/ita_fr.htm

B-C

Baden Air	http://www.badenair.de
Balair/CTA	http://www.gotravel.com/balair/index.html
Balkan Bulgarian Airlines	http://www.balkanair.com
Bellview Airlines	http://www.bellviewairlines.nl
Braathens	http://www.braathens.no
Britannia Airways	http://www.britanniaairways.com
British Airways	http://www.british-airways.com

British Midland	http://www.iflybritishmidland.com
Buzz	http://www.buzzaway.com
City Bird Airlines	http://www.citybird.com
Condor Airlines	http://www.condor.de
Corsair	http://www.corsair-int.com
Croatia Airlines	http://www.ctn.tel.hr/ctn
Crossair	http://www.crossair.com
CSA Czech Airlines	http://www.baxter.net/csa/csa_fra.html

D-G

Denim Airways	http://www.denimair.nl
Deutsche BA	http://www.deutsche-ba.de
EasyJet	http://www.easyjet.com
Eurowings	http://www.eurowings.de/main_e.html
Falcon Air	http://www.falconair.se
Finnair	http://www.finnair.fi
Flying Enterprise	http://www.flying.se
Gandalf Airlines	http://www.gandalfair.com/index.htm
GB Airways	http://www.gbairways.gi
Germania Airlines	http://www.germaniaairline.de
Go Airlines	http://www.go-fly.com
Greenlandair	http://www.greenland-guide.dk/gla/default.htm

H-L

Hamburg International	http://www.hamburg-international.de
Hapag-Lloyd Flug	http://www.hlf.de
Hungarian Airlines	http://www.travelfirst.com/pays/hungo_e.html
Iberia Airlines	http://www.iberia.com
Icelandair	http://www.icelandair.is
Istanbul Airlines	http://www.ihy.com.tr
JAT Yugoslav Airlines	http://www.jat.com
Jersey European Airways	http://www.jerseyeuropean.co.uk
KLM	http://www.klm.nl
KLM UK	http://www.airuk.co.uk
Korsar	http://www.olvit.iasnet.ru/transpor/korcar/in.htm
Lauda Air	http://www.laudaair.com
LOT Polish Airlines	http://www.lot.com
LTU	http://www.ltu.com
Lufthansa	http://www.lufthansa.com
Luxair	http://www.luxair.lu

M-S

Maersk Air	http://www.maersk-air.com

Malev Hungarian Airlines	http://www.malev.hu
Manx Airlines	http://www.manx-airlines.com
MaxAir	http://www.maxair.com
Med Air	http://www.medairlines.it/Default2.htm
Meridiana	http://www.meridiana.it
Monarch Airlines	http://www.monarch-airlines.com
Olympic Airways	http://www.olympic-airways.gr
Portugalia Airways	http://www.pga.pt
Pulkovo Airlines	http://www.pulkovo.ru/english/airline/default.asp
Regional Airlines	http://www.regionalairlines.com
Rhientalflug	http://www2.vol.at/rheintalflug
RIAir Riga	http://www.riga-airlines.com
Ryan Air	http://www.ryanair.ie
Sabena	http://www.sabena.com
SAS	http://www.flysas.com
SATA Air Acores	http://www.virtualazores.com/sata/en/index.html
Skyways	http://www.skyways.se
Spanair	http://www.spanair.com/es
Suckling Airways	http://ds.dial.pipex.com/suckling.airways
Swiss World Airways	http://altern.org/swa
Swissair	http://www.swissair.com

T-Z

TAP Air Portugal	http://www.tap.pt/en
TAROM Romanian Air Transport	http://tarom.digiro.net
Tempelhof Express	http://www.tempelhof-express.com
Transwede	http://www.transwede.se
TTA	http://www.tta.nl/tta.html
Turkish Airlines	http://www.turkishairlines.com
Tyrolean	http://www.telecom.at/aua/tyrolean
Virgin Atlantic	http://www.fly.virgin.com
Virgin Express	http://www.virgin-exp.com
Volare Airlines	http://www.volare-airlines.com
Volga Dnepr Airlines	http://www.voldn.ru
WestJet Airlines	http://www.westjet.com
Wideroe	http://www.wideroe.no

United States and Canadian Airlines

A-B

Air Alaska	http://www.alaska-air.com
Air Canada	http://www.aircanada.ca
Air Labrador	http://www.airlabrador.com

Air Ontario	http://www.airontario.com
Air Transat	http://www.airtransat.com
Airborne Express	http://www.airborne-express.com
AirNova	http://www.airnova.ca/Englis
Airtran Airways	http://www.airtran.com
Aloha Airlines	http://www.alohaair.com
America West Airlines	http://www.americawest.com
American Airlines	http://www.aa.com
American Trans Air	http://www.ata.com
Atlantic Coast Airlines	http://www.atlanticcoast.com
Atlas Air	http://www.atlasair.com
Austin Express	http://www.austinexpress.com
Big Sky Airlines	http://www.bigskyair.com
Burlington Air Express	http://www.baxworld.com
Business Express Airlines	http://www.bexair.com

C-D

California Coastal Airways	http://www.aviationworldservices.com/cca.htm
Calm Air	http://www.calmair.com
Canada 3000	http://www.canada3000.com
Canadian Airlines	http://www.cdnair.ca
Cardinal Airlines	http://www.flycardinal.com
Casino Express	http://www.redlioncasino.com/CasinoExpress/index.html
Champion Air	http://www.championair.com
Chautauqua Airlines	http://www.flychautauqua.com/home.html
Chicago Express	http://www.chicagoexpress.com
Colgan Air	http://www.colganair.com
Comair	http://comair.com
Continental Airlines	http://www.continental.com
Crystal Airways	http://www.crystalairways.com/index.html
Delta Airlines	http://www.delta-air.com/index.html
Delta Express	http://www.delta-air.com/express/index.html
DHL Worldwide Express	http://www.dhl.com

E-M

Emery Worldwide	http://www.emeryworld.com
Era Aviation	http://www.era-aviation.com
Evergreen Aviation	http://www.evergreenaviation.com
FedEx	http://www.fedex.com
Fine Air	http://www.fineair.com
First Air	http://www.firstair.ca
Frontier Airlines	http://www.flyfrontier.com
Great Lakes Aviation	http://www.greatlakesav.com

Gulfstream Airlines	http://www.gulfstreamair.com
Hawiian Airlines	http://www.hawaiianair.com
Horizon Air	http://www.horizonair.com
Kitty Hawk	http://www.kha.com
Mesa Air Group	http://www.mesa-air.com
Mesaba Airlines	http://www.mesaba.com
MetroJet	http://www.flymetrojet.com
Miami Air	http://www.miamiair.com
Midway Airlines	http://www.midwayair.com
Midwest Express Airlines	http://www.midwestexpress.com
Mountain Air Express	http://www.mountainairexpress.com

N-T

Nation Air Express	http://www.nationsair.com
National Airlines	http://www.nationalairlines.com
North Vancouver Air	http://www.northvanair.com
Northwest Airlines	http://www.nwa.com
Pacific Coastal Airlines	http://www.pacific-coastal.com/home.htm
Piedmont Airlines	http://www.piedmont-airlines.com
Pro Air	http://www.proair.com
Royal Air	http://www.royalair.com/e-neuf.htm
Skyservice Airlines	http://www.skyserviceairlines.com
Skywest	http://www.skywest.com
Southwest Airlines	http://www.iflyswa.com
Spirit Airlines	http://www.spiritair.com
Star Alliance	http://www.star-alliance.com
Sun Country Airlines	http://www.suncountry.com
SunJet	http://www.sunjet.com
Tahoe Air	http://www.tahoeair.com
Tower Air	http://www.towerair.com
Tran States Airlines	http://www.transstates.net
TWA	http://www.twa.com

U-Z

United Airlines	http://www.ual.com
US Airways	http://www.usairways.com
Vanguard	http://www.flyvanguard.com
West Jet	http://www.westjet.com
World Airways	http://www.worldair.com

Middle East Airlines

A-Z

Arkia Israeli Airlines	http://www.arkia.co.il
Bhoja Air	http://www.jamals.com/bhoja/index.htm
Cyprus Airways	http://www.cyprusair.com
Egypt Air	http://www.powerup.com.au/~ancient/eair1.htm
El Al	http://www.elal.co.il
Emirates	http://www.ekgroup.com
Gulf Air	http://www.gulfairco.com
Iran Air	http://www.aeolos.com/iranair.htm
Middle East Airlines	http://www.mea.com.lb
Orca Air	http://www.orca-air.com
Qatar Airways	http://qatarairways.com/qr
Royal Air Maroc	http://www.kingdomofmorocco.com/html/royal_air.html
Royal Jordanian Airline	http://www.rja.com.jo
Royal Wings Airlines	http://www.royalwings.com.jo
Saudi Arabian Airlines	http://www.saudiairlines.com
Yemen Airways	http://home.earthlink.net/~yemenair

Asian and Pacific Airlines

A-B

Air Asia	http://www.airasia.com
Air Caledonie International	http://www.pacificislands.com/airlines/caledonie.html
Air China	http://www.airchina.com.cn
Air Fiji	http://www.pacificislands.com/airlines/fiji.html
Air India	http://www.airindia.com
Air Lanka	http://www.airlanka.com
Air Mandalay	http://www.air-mandalay.com
Air Nauru	http://www.airnauru.com.au
Air New Zealand	http://airnz.com
Air Niugini	http://www.airniugini.com.pg
Air Rarotonga	http://www.ck/edairaro.htm
Air Vanuatu	http://www.pacificislands.com/airlines/vanuatu.html
All Nipon Airways	http://www.ana.co.jp
Ansett Australia	http://www.ansett.com.au

Asiana Airlines	http://www.asiana.co.kr
Bangkok Airways	http://www.bkkair.co.th
Biman Bangladesh Airlines	http://www.bangladeshonline.com/biman
Bouraq Indonesia Airlines	http://www.bouraq.com

C-O

Cathay Pacific	http://www.cathaypacific.com
China Airlines	http://www.cyberconnect.com/formosa/CI/ci.htm
China Southern Airlines	http://203.127.117.130
China Southwest Airlines	http://www.cswa.com
Continental Micronesia	http://www.destmic.com
Dragon Air	http://www.dragonair.com
Druk Air	http://www.taurusair.com/bhutan/druk-air.htm
Eva Airways	http://www.evaair.com.tw/english/index.htm
Flight West	http://www.fltwest.com.au
Freedom Air	http://www.freedomair.co.nz
GMG Airlines	http://www.gmggroup.com
Indian Airlines	http://www.nic.in/indian-airlines
Japan Airlines	http://www.jal.co.jp
Korean Air	http://www.koreanair.com
Malaysian Airlines	http://www.malaysia-airlines.com
Mandarin Airlines	http://www.mandarin-airlines.com
Mongolia Airlines	http://www.arpnet.it/~mongolia/viaggi/aereo.htm

P-Z

Pakistan International Airlines	http://www.piac.com/index.htm
Philippine Airlines	http://www.philippineair.com
Polynesian Airlines	http://www.pacificislands.com/airlines/polynesian.html
Qantas Airways	http://www.qantas.com.au
Royal Tongan Airlines	http://kalianet.candw.to/rta
Sahara India Airlines	http://www.saharaairline.com
Shandong Airlines	http://www.sh.com
Si Chuan Airlines	http://info.scsti.ac.cn/English/eco/air.html
Singapore Airlines	http://www.singaporeair.com
Skymark Airlines	http://www.skymark.co.jp
Skywest Airlines	http://www.skywest.com.au
Solomon Airlines	http://www.pacificislands.com/airlines/solomon.html
Spirit Airlines	http://www.spiritairlines.com.au
Thai Airways International	http://www.thaiairways.com

African Airlines

A-Z

Air Afrique	http://www.sinergia.it/airafrique.htm
Air Mauritius	http://www.airmauritius.com
Air Namibia	http://www.airnamibia.com.na
Air Zimbabwe	http://www.airzimbabwe.com
Alliance Airlines	http://www.baxter.net/alliance
Daallo Airlines	http://www.daallo.com
Ethiopian Airlines	http://www.ethiopianairlines.com
Expedition Airways	http://www.africaonline.co.zw/expedition
Interair	http://rapidttp.com/travel/br/zinterai.html
Kenya Airways	http://www.kenyaairways.co.uk
Nouvelair	http://www.nouvelair.com
PrecisionAir	http://www.precisionairtz.com
South African Airways	http://www.saa.co.za
South African Express	http://www.saexpress.co.za/index5.html
Tunisair	http://www.tunisair.com.tn
Uganda	http://www.imul.com/uganda/qu.html
Zimbabwe Express Airways	http://rapidttp.com/travel/br/zzimexpr.html

South American and Latin Airlines

A-B

ACES Colombia	http://www.acescolombia.com
Aero Caribe	http://www.aerocaribe.com
Aero Continente	http://200.4.197.130
Aero Costa Rica	http://www.centralamerica.com/cr/tran/aero.htm
Aerolineas Argentinas	http://www.aerolineas.com.ar
Aeroliners Internacionales	http://www.iwm.com.mx/foroemp/aerint.html
AeroLitoral	http://www.aerolitoral.com.mx
Aeromar	http://www.aeromar-air.com
Aeromexico	http://www.aeromexico.com
Air ALM	http://www.airalm.com
Air Aruba	http://www.interknowledge.com/air-aruba
Air Caribbean	http://www.sputnick.com/aircaribbean
Air Jamaica	http://www.airjamaica.com
Aserca Airlines	http://www.asercaairlines.com
Austral Lineas	http://www.austral.com.ar
Avensa	http://www.avensa.com.ve
Aviateca	http://www.grupotaca.com
Bahamasair	http://www.bahamasair.com

British West Indies Airways   http://www.bwiacaribbean.com

C-S
Cayman Airways   http://cayman.com.ky/com/cal/index.htm
Copa   http://www.flylatinamerica.com
Cubana de Aviacion   http://www.cubana.cu
Groupo Taca   http://www.grupotaca.com
Guyana Airways   http://www.turq.com/guyana/guyanair.html
Intercontinental de Aviacon http://www.insite-network.com/Inter
LACSA   http://www.grupotaca.com
Ladeco   http://www.ladeco.com
LanChile   http://www.lanchile.com
LIAT   http://www.candoo.com/liat
Lynx Air   http://www.lynxair.com
Maya Airways   http://www.mayaairways.com
Mexicana Airlines   http://www.mexicana.com/index.html
NICA   http://www.grupotaca.com
Nordeste Linas Ae'reas   http://www.nordeste.com
Pantanal Linhas Aereas   http://www.pantanal-airlines.com.br
Rio-Sul   http://www.rio-sul.com

T-Z
Taca International Airlines http://www.grupotaca.com
Taesa   http://www.taesa.com.mx
Tam Airlines   http://www.tam.com.br
Tame   http://wwwpub4.ecua.net.ec/tame
Total Air   http://www.total.com.br
Transair International   http://www.transair.com.br
TransBrasil   http://www.transbrasil.com.br
TravelAir   http://www.centralamerica.com/cr/tran/travlair.htm
Varig   http://www.varig.com.br
Vasp   http://www.vasp.com.br

Whilst every effort has been made to check these web site addresses, there will on occasions be 'dead links', either because the web site has ceased operation or the company in question has altered their web site address. If you come across any, please send an e-mail to the following address naming the dead link.

andrewdporter@yahoo.co.uk